The Leader and His or Her Performance

The Leader and His or Her Performance

DR. RAYMOND SAINTIL

ARPress
ILLUMINATING IDEAS
EMPOWERING VOICES

ARPress
45 Dan Road Suite 5
Canton MA 02021

Hotline: 1(888) 821-0229
Fax: 1(508) 545-7580

Ordering Information:
Quantity sales. Special discounts are available on quantity purchases by corporations, associations, and others. For details, contact the publisher at the address above.

Printed in the United States of America.

ISBN-13:   Softcover   979-8-89389-883-5
            eBook   979-8-89389-884-2

Library of Congress Control Number: 979-8-89389-884-2

Table of Contents

PREFACE

This book is written for the use of colleges, Universities, Businessmen, Evangelical Leaders, Entrepreneurs, Industries and other. This book describes something very important about Managers, Supervisors, Evangelical Leaders, and Entrepreneurs etc. The readers may pay attention when they Read this important Book for their interest in the Market-Place.

CHAPTER 1
THE LEADER AND HIS/HER PERFORMANCE

INTRODUCTION: HOW THE LEADER CAN INSPIRE HIS EMPLOYEES IN ORDER TO GIVE THE BEST PERFORMANCE?

First of all, working is a condition Sine qua non demanding by God for every Nation. We all know that Happy workers are more likely to stay with the industry, take good care of customers and do what their Patron needs sometimes it may feel like developing engaged employees is impossible. However, Satisfied workers don't have to be mythical creatures, sighted as frequently as unicorns in the forest. With care and hard work, we can create a work-place environment that support worker happiness. And, it may not be as difficult as we think. The key is for us to recognize the difference between being a manager and being a Leader. The Role of the Manager is to plan, organize, assign, and follow up. What about the Leader himself?

The Leader himself needs to influence, Motivate and encourage. Our job as company supervisor Requires us to excel at both skills to be successful. But the Leadership component means us must Build good relationships with employees in order to influence, motivate and encourage (Alban-Metcalfe, R.J., & Alimo-Metcalfe, B. (2000).

LET US SPEAK ABOUT A LEADER WITH A GOOD PERFORMANCE!

How can leadership improve performance? how can we as our leader support us with our performance? How do we inspire employees to give their best performance?

In certain sense that leadership strategies that influence, engage and encourage excellent performance.

Can you define and communicate vision? Certainly, we can say that the eye looks, but it is the Mind that sees. Encourage recognition, employees want to feel appreciated.

- Speak from the heart
- Delegate and Empower
- Commit to Continued Education

LEADERSHIP STRATEGIES TO IMPROVE TEAM PERFORMANCE

Still, we can start supporting our Team today with these strong leadership habits.

1. Look at the Picture
2. Be Decisive and confident
3. Prioritize what is truly important
4. Build on your strengths
5. Build on the strengths of others

6. Empower and inspire others
7. Practice Optimism
8. Communicate, Communicate, Communicate.

How do you provide leadership? here are five strategies, vital to developing employee leadership skills, that will benefit employers and employees alike:

1. Encourage employees to network
2. Act as a Mentor (or assign one)
3. Provide opportunities for growth
4. Maintain a feedback loop
5. Lead by Example

What Makes an Effective Leader?

1. Passion

An effective leader is a person with passion for a cause that is larger than they are Holder of Values

LEADERSHIP IMPLIES VALUES

- Vision
- Creativity
- Intellectual drive and humility combined
- Communicator
- Planner/Organizer

The impact of Leadership on organizational performance Leadership skills are not tangible, while many leaders are born with a specific leadership Ability, anybody can learn to improve their leadership skills. Through self-awareness and Training, you can boost the impact you have on your Team, which often has a tangible Effect on performance (Borman, W.C., & Brush, D.H. (1993).

Here are some examples on tangible Effective on performance

1. Employee Training
2. Performance Management for Employee
3. Leadership skills (Chan, D. W. (2003).

What are the objectives of leadership? & Leadership qualities?

As a small business leader, your most important objective is to run a successful business; but for your business to succeed; your employees must also succeed, both in their individual functions and as a Team. Your objective as a leader must be to inspire your employees to pull together toward shared business goals. To attain this objective, you must acquire certain leadership skills.

- Objective of Leadership
- Leadership Skills
- Organizational Chart
- Leadership Styles
- Employee Motivation

Would you define objectives?

Before a business owner can lead others, he / she must first learn who he/ she is and What he / she wants his/ her business to accomplish. A leader should make a list of Specific, realistic goals, he/she wants his / her business to achieve, then prioritize Them. Every business leader wants his/ her company to be profitable, but he/ she usually wants it to be something else as well.

A leader should clearly articulate to himself what his /her secondary goals are, and when they take priority over the primary goals of profit, growth is one common Secondary goal you may decide to run a bargain basement sale to acquire new customers, or sacrifice short-term profit by spending on expansion. However, an owner may also have non-monetary goals for his/her business, which also need to be clearly defined for example, helping the poor may be an important part of an owner's religious beliefs. Therefore, corporate donations to a homeless shelter may take precedence over making the highest possible profits. An owner may retrofit his/her office with "green "materials to be environmentally responsible, even though it costs more in the short-term. If you have more than one goal as a business leader. It is important to make it clear to your employees. After all, it is hard for them to follow you if they cannot see where you are going.

Communication Objectives There are 9 examples of communication objectives. We define that communication objectives are goals for messages or programs of Communication. They are used to identify your audience, craft messages and evaluate results. Communication objectives is a broad term that can apply to areas such as marketing, sales, knowledge work, create works, public speaking, governance, management and leadership. The following are illustrative examples of communication objectives. Arnold, J. a., Arad, S., Rhoades, J.A., & Drasgow, F. (2000).

LEADERSHIP

Getting people moving in the same direction to achieve goal. For example, reducing Resistance to change.

MOTIVATION

Motivating people to improve results such as productivity

KNOWLEDGE

Conveying knowledge, for example, a training objective that everyone understands Several foundational concepts at the end of a session.

What do you mean by influence?

Influencing actions, for example, an employee with an objective to change a Team's strategy.

What about Persuasion?

Persuasion is selling an idea, for example, a public speaker who would like to change Minds about a particular topic.
Entertainment

Entertaining is an audience with music, art, humor or storytelling.

What do you mean by Demand generation?

Demand generation is an interest in a product or service.

What about Brand Awareness?

Brand awareness is developing brand recognition and brand awareness such as top of Mind.

TRANSACTION: Getting to yes to close as a sale or partnership-agreement. Brand recognition is the extent to which the public can correctly identify products and services by their brand including factors such as logo, Color, Slogan or style. In many cases, Customers are more likely to choose a brand they have heard of, even if they know Nothing about it.

What do you say about Calculation?

A calculation is a brand recognition that evaluated by showing customers the visual symbols of your brand such as a logo, package or product and testing if they can identify it. This can be measured us the percentage of people who recognize your brand symbols. Brand recognition is equal number of customers who recognize brand / number of customers asked) x 100. For example, a chair restaurant asks 30 customers to identify the brand's logo. The logo is mixed in with other brand logos to reduce lucky guesses.

A total of 8 customers can correctly identify the logo. Brand recognition is equal (8/30) x 100 = 26.6 % you have arrived. That's why it's so important to create objectives that can be measured using research tools like surveys and web analytics. By creating specific, measurable objectives, you will be able to answer the question "are we there yet?" With a precise response: yes!

COMMUNICATING PROJECT GOALS TO YOUR TEAM MEMBERS

1. Set motivating goals. Before you can communicate goals with your project Team, you need to set them first. 2- The Method, there are many ways to communicate goals: you can convey them via a formal document or direct communication.
2. Be Confident
3. Communicate Clear Expectations
4. On going Dialogue
5. Rinse and Repeat

What are Team Roles?

Team Roles are Team members who have been selected because they have particular Skills that are required to complete project tasks. Examples include specialists in business or Technical, disciplines, or an outside supplier. The Role often requires Team members to work on their own initiative in areas where they are the expects.

Tell us about Communications objectives?

Communication objectives is an intended goals of an advertising or promotional Program. Possible communications objectives include:

1. Creative Awareness
2. Imparting Knowledge
3. Projecting an image
4. Shaping Attitudes
5. Stimulating a want or desire, and/or
6. Effecting a sale.

What about popular terms?

Popular terms are attributed to Marketing, distribution change, marketing strategy, Product, receiving, marketing mix, marked orientation, market equilibration.

Tell us about the Distribution channel?

In the distribution channel it is concerned about the path through which goals and services travel from the vendor to the consumer or payment for those products travel from the consumer to the vendor. A distribution Channel can be as short as a direct transaction from the vendor to the consumer or may include several interconnected inter diaries along the way such as whole sales, distributors, agents and retailers. Each intermediary receives the item at one pricing point and moving it to the next higher pricing point until it reaches the final buyer. Coffee does not reach the consumer before first going through a channel involving the farmer, importer, distributor and the retailer.

CHAPTER 2
HOW TO DISTINGUISH A PERFORMANCE EVALUATION?

The performance of an individual, based on pre-determine standards. On the other hand, performance management alludes to the management of performance of the manpower working in an organization. While performance appraisal is a yearly system while if we talk about performance management it is a continuous process that does not occur eventually. What kind of evaluation process is adopted by the organization is one of the biggest questions, as the appreciation and development of employees rely on it? Some employees work silently but does not show himself/herself, while there are also, such employees who put up a show but hardly performs. So, the performance appraisal and management play a crucial role, as the success of the organization is combined effort of all the employees and the entrepreneur.

Of course, we persuade on definition of performance management in all forms. For Instance, by definition of the performance management it is a continuous process that Aims at planning. Monitoring and evaluating the objectives of an employees and his total contribution to the organization. The basic purpose of performance management is to encourage and improve employee's efficiency and effectiveness. In this process, both the employees and the managers participate in setting the objectives. Assessing the performance or progress, providing training and feedback to the employees at regular intervals for improvement, implementing development programs for employees and rewarding them for their achievements. (Allen T., & Bronte-Tinkew, (2008, January). With the help of this process, both the employee and the employer get a chance to set the combined. Screen is a sample of what an evaluation would look like.

PERFORMANCE APPRAISAL

Evaluating the performance and potential of employees typically to determine compensation.

PERFORMANCE MANAGEMENT

Managing and developing employee performance to foster growth with the Organization.

SCOPE OF EXECUTION

There are some similarities between the terms when it comes to execution. Both performance appraisal and performance management involve:

1. Setting targets and clear expectation
2. Setting guidelines measuring success
3. Reviewing whether targets were achieved
4. Identifying barriers towards effective performance
5. Determining ways to help employees meet these targets

Frequently Performance appraisal is a reactive function that only evaluates past performance of employees in most organizations, it is usually conducted only once or twice in a Year. It is a distinct staff activity doesn't interfere with an employee's daily work. Performance management is a proactive, toward looking process that manages

Employee performance in an ongoing manner, the intent here is to make sure Employees attain their targets in real time. Ideally there shouldn't be a need for Corrective action if the goals have been set according to the employee's Potential. This process does make a difference to how employees carry on with their daily tasks. Many forward-looking companies have made performance Appraisal a part of their performance management process. It has helped them to Take corrective action and assign further targets by combining the two.

Performance management involves both employees and their line managers. Additionally other stake-holders do play an important role. These other stakeholders can be any one who can positively impact employee's performance customize the process according to each individual employee's behavioral work. (Rao, T. V. (1985). Performance appraisal is typically a standard procedure conducted by the HR department in collaboration with direct managers. It depends upon the employee's designation, experience and job description. Here, more often than not the supervisor or manager plays the role of a judge and has final work. Some companies, there are appraisal systems that allow setting up of joint targets by the employee and their managers. You can also evaluate them on frequently which is why they appear the similar to performance management.

The only problem is that they are not able to monitor budgets in real-time, a Comfort offered by the performance management process.

STRUCTURE

Even though the performance appraisal process is more structured and formal, it Does allow customization of the key performance areas which vary from employee to employee. However, when it comes to setting rating parameters, it is quite Rigid as these ratings are applicable for every employee. In contrast, the performance management process is quite flexible at evaluating performance.

While there are certain guidelines that optimal performance. They can vary from Employee to employee depending on their job description and capabilities. We can See that performance appraisal is, in a way, an essential process that goes along Well with performance management. It is safe to say that performance appraisal Is just one piece of the larger puzzle of performance management. What is the Different between performance appraisal and performance evaluation? We can say That performance appraisal, on the other hand, is the ongoing. Process of Evaluating employee performance. Another way to think of the difference between the two is that performance appraisal is about the past, meaning how the Employee performed in the immediate past period being recapitulated during the Appraisal process. Craig, S.E., Beauty. R.W., & Baird, L.S. (1986).

HOW DO YOU EVALUATE SYSTEM PERFORMANCE?

PERFORMANCE EVALUATION SYSTEM (PES)

CLASSIFIED EMPLOYEES

The performance evaluation system is a used to measure individual performance and to develop employees into high-performing individuals. It applies to all classified employees and the current system is effective in the year of 2012. Which is (7/1/2012). To create a performance evaluation system in your practice, follow these five steps:

1. Develop an evaluation form
2. Identify performance measures
3. Set guidelines for feedback
4. Create disciplinary and termination procedures
5. Set an evaluation schedule

What are the Methods of performance evaluation?

We can say that employee performance evaluation methods are defined as the Techniques used to judge a particular employee's work performance in order to give him or her the benefits of the job. There are many things which depend on these methods like an employee's appraisal, performance recapitulation, and career development. (Monga, M.L. (1983).

What are the benefits of performance appraisal?

Performance appraisal allows you to provide positive feedback as well identifying Areas for improvement. An employee can discuss and even create a developmental (training) plan with the manager so he can improve his skills. It motivates Employees if supported by a good merit-based compensation system. (Moore, K.A. 2008, January).

UNILATERAL CONTRACT

In a unilateral contract, the promisor makes an open promise to provide something in exchange for performance.

What about a bilateral contract?

In a bilateral contract, both the promisor and the promise knowingly enter into an Agreement where both parties make a promise, and each is obligated to fulfill the Promise. It is very important to redress the difference between performance Appraisal and performance management. In this oblique of facts, performance Appraisal implies a rational assessment of communicate clear expectations, ongoing dialogue, Rinse and repeat.

What are Team Roles?

The Team members are selected because they have particular skills that are Required to complete project tasks. Examples include specialists in business or Technical, disciplines, or an outside supplier. The role often requires team Members to work on their own initiative in areas where they are the expects.

Communication Objectives

Intended goals of an advertising or promotional program. Possible communications objectives include:

1. Create awareness
2. Imparting knowledge
3. Projecting an image
4. Shaping attitudes
5. Stimulating a want or desire, and/or
6. Effecting a Sale

What are Popular Terms?

The popular terms are a marketing, distribution change, marketing strategy, Product, receiving, marketing mix, marked orientation, market equilibration.

What you mean by distribution channel?

The distribution channel is the path through which goals and services travel from the vendor to the consumer or payment for those products travel from the Consumer to the vendor. A distribution channel can be as short as a direct transaction from the vendor to the consumer or may include several Interconnected interne diaries along the way such as whole sales, distributors, Agents and retailers. Each intermediary receives the item at one pricing point and moves it to the next higher pricing point until it reaches the final buyer. Coffee Does not reach the consumer before first going through a channel involving the Farmer, importer, distributor and the retailer. (Patten, T. H., Jr. (1982).

PERFORMANCE EVALUATION

HOW DO YOU DEFINE THE PERFORMANCE EVALUATION OF A GOOD LEADER?

The performance evaluation of a good Leader is defined as a formal and productive procedure to measure an employee's job responsibilities. It is used to gauge the amount of value added by an employee in terms of increased business revenue, in comparison to industry standards and overall employee return on investment (Roi). All organizations that have learned the art of "winning from within "by focusing inward towards their employees, rely on a systematic performance evaluation process to regularly measure and evaluate employee performance. Ideally, employees are graded annually on their work anniversaries on the basis of which, they are either promote or suitable distribution of salary raises. We can say that performance evaluation also plays a direct role in providing periodic feedback to employees, such that they are more self-aware in terms of their own performance metrics.

What is the purpose of Performance Evaluation?

The purpose of Performance Evaluation is:

1. Periodic performance evaluation is an employee's report card from his / her manager that Acknowledges the work he/she has done in a specific time period and the scope for improvement.
2. An employer can provide consistent feedback on an employee's strengths and strive for Improvement in the areas that the employees need to work on.
3. It is an integral platform for both, the employee and employer, to attain a common ground on What both think is benefitting a quality performance. This helps in improving communication Which usually leads to better and more

accurate Team metrics and thus, improved performance results.

4. The good of this entire process of performance evaluation is to improve the way a team or an organization function, to achieve higher levels of customer satisfaction.

5. A manager should evaluate his/her Team member regularly and not just once a year. This way the team can avert new and unexpected problems with constant work being done to improve Competence and efficiency.

6. An organization's management can conduct frequent employee training and skill development Sessions on the basis of the development areas recognized after a performance evaluation session.

7. The management can effectively manage the Team and conduct productive resource Allocation after evaluating the goals and preset standards of performance.

8. Regular performance evaluation can help determine the scope of growth in an employee's Career and the level of motivation with which he/she contributes towards the success of an organization.

PERFORMANCE EVALUATION

"Why" makes a difference? Here are the key points:

1. People providing performance evaluation ratings for salary or promotion purposes tend to be more generous and less accurate than when providing ratings for development or Feedback purposes.

2. Like guardians who always think their children are above average, the generous effect on salary and promotion decisions.

3. Prosperous "framework of reference's training, rating scales based on specific Behaviors, and improving raters'

motivation and accountability can all help to reduce the Effect s of over generous ratings. Assuming that you design or develop performance Evaluation systems, then changes are you are aware of the problems in getting managers and employees to evaluate performance accurately. Nevertheless, of whether the problem Is getting raters to recognize poor performance, or getting them to rate it more accurately, Bias is an issue. (Riot. V.(1985)

PERFORMANCE EVALUATION RATINGS

In particular, people providing ratings for salary or promotion purposes tend to be more Generous and less accurate than they are when rating employee development or giving Feedback. It seems that in the real word, raters don't like to mark people down, and they Don't like to make big distinction in performance between people. This means that, like guardians being asked to rate their own children, most people end up being above average. Since it was a consistent finding over a large number of people, it importunes an obvious investigation. Employees also can provide valuable feedback on their managers, spotting potential areas of weakness to be addressed with advanced, potentially one-on-one training sessions.

PERFORMANCE STANDARDS

Performance standards meaning is to describe what you want workers in a particular job to accomplish and how you want the job done. These standards apply across the board, to every employee who holds the same position. For example, a performance standard for a sales person might be to make $60,000 in sales per quarter. Make sure your standards are achievable and directly related to the employee's job.

GOALS

What you mean about GOALS?

Contrary performance standards, goals should be tailored to each employee; they will Depend on the individual worker's strengths and weaknesses. For example; a goal for a Graphic artist might be learning a new software program that will make his or her work more efficient; for an accounting professional a goal might be to take the exam to become a certified accountant public, your workers can help figure out what goals are reasonable and appropriate. Once you have defined the standards and goals for each position and worker, write them down and hand them out to your employees. This will let your employees know what you expect and what they will have to achieve during the year to achieve during the year to receive a positive evaluation.

CONTRIBUTING THE EVALUATION

At least once a year, formally evaluate each employee by writing a performance recapitulation and holding a meeting with the employee. To prepare, gather and recapitulate all of the documents and records relating to the employee's performance, productivity, and behavior. Retrospect your mark and the employee's personnel file.

You might also want to take a look at other company records relating to the worker, including sales records, call reports, productivity records, time cards, or budget reports. Once you have recapitulated these documents and gathered your thoughts about the employee's work, write the performance audit. Although a performance analysis can take many forms, it should include:

1. Each standard or goal you set for that worker and that job.
2. Your conclusion as to whether the employee met the standard or goal and...

3. The reasons that support your conclusion. If you will solicit input from other managers, ask each of them to complete an evaluation, and then compile them. You might also want the employee to conduct a self-evaluation in advance of the meeting. Remember, whenever you have finished writing the evaluation, set up a meeting to discuss it with the employee. Remember, this is likely to be one of the most important meetings you have with each issue thoroughly. At the meeting let your workers know what you think he or she did well and which areas could use some improvement. Using your evaluations as a guide, explain your conclusions about each standard and goal. Listen carefully to your worker's comments and ask the worker to write them down on the evaluation form. Take notes on the meeting and include those notes on the form.

PERFORMANCE STANDARDS

Performance standards describe what you want workers in a particular job to accomplish and how you Want the job done. These standards apply across the board, to every employee who holds the same position. For example, a performance standard for a sales person might be to make $50,000 in sales per quarter. Make sure your standards are achievable and directly related to the employee's job.

GOALS OF EMPLOYEE PERFORMANCE EVALUATION

The goals of best employee performance evaluation also include employee development and Organizational improvement. The goal of employee performance evaluation is to create accurate Appraisal documentation to protect both the employee and the employer.

How do you write a work performance goal?

In order to set smart goals, it is important to understand what productivity, development, and Professional goals: Relate to the position at hand. Focus on the duties of the job and what it produces?

What are Smart Goals?

1. Specific
2. Measurable
3. Attainable
4. Relevant
5. Time Sensitive

CHAPTER 3

MEASURING AND MANAGING INDIVIDUAL PRODUCTIVITY

A s important as productivity is to the continued economic development of the world, it is surprising that so little is known about measuring and managing it. Part of the problem may lie in the unit of analysis industry uses to measure Productivity and, in a failure, to recognize the complexity of the relationship Between the productivity of the individual worker and the total performance of the organization. In this contrast, the body of research knowledge provides little help. A multitude of micro studies of individual work behavior exist, but the measure of productivity used is seldom comparable to those developed in industry. Organizational studies generally focus on the total performance of the organization, but even those that are centered on organizational productivity rarely attempt to disaggregate findings to the business unit, work group, or individual level in any systematic way. In a general sense, the productivity of the world is a function of the productivity of each of the world's economics; the economics, in turn, are as productive as the organizations within them. Within the organization, individual workers performing specific jobs form the base Level for all productive endeavor. In modern, complex organizations, however, the linkage between individual productivity and the productivity of organizational

Systems becomes blurred. For a variety of reasons, the linkages are seldom one to one. Only by understanding the individual level of productivity, however, can Practitioners and researchers begin to build the theories and models that deal with the dysfunctions and synergies that occur when individuals are grouped into work Teams, departments organizations are set in the context of a changing, competitive, environment in which strategies are developed to guide the efforts of management and workers toward a common vision and set of objectives. Even the best designed processes will fail without a supportive culture within the organization that values change, continuous improvement, goal commitment, Group cohesion, and respect for people. Every concept in this chapter assumes that the individual worker and the work group are set in an organizational context that is internally consistent and environmentally consonant. It is also important to note that productivity, although a major concern, is not the only indicator of individual or organizational performance. Productivity interacts with other aspects of employee performance, financial controls, innovation, and competitive effectiveness, any one of which can lead to organizational failure. In this chapter sink and Smith identify seven related but separable performance criteria for an organizational system:

1. Effectiveness
2. Efficiency
3. Productivity
4. Quality
5. Quality of working life
6. Innovation, and
7. Profitability (Profit Center). Or budget ability (Cost Center).

For the purposes of this chapter, my definition of productivity includes effectiveness (producing the right products or services), efficiency (prudent utilization of resources), and quality (meeting technical and customer specifications). My purpose in this chapter is to assimilate knowledge about the measurement and management of individual productivity in order to provide a link in the chain of understanding regarding how individual productivity contributes to organizational productivity. My intent is to aggregate existing knowledge and propose some theoretical foundations in order to reveal areas and empirical research are needed.

Throughout, I make an effort to bridge the gap between the concerns of Researchers and industry. (Cooper, R., and R.S. Kaplan. (1991).

PRODUCTIVITY MEASUREMENT AND GOAL ALIGNMENT

In industry, the measurement and analysis of individual-level productivity serves The following five major functions:

1. Define productivity and direct behavior: the measurement system provides An implicit definition of productivity for the operation. It communicates to the Worker, the supervisor, and others the common expectation from the task. The productivity measurement provides specific direction and guides the Worker toward productive activities.

2. Monitor performance and provide Feedback: the measurement system provides a means to check progress Toward an objective. In addition, it can be a major part of the employee's Performance evaluation leading to rewards or disciplinary action.

3. Diagnose Problems; productivity analysis, particularly the examination of trends, helps Identify problems before they become crises and permits early adjustment and Corrective action. Like any other indicator, productivity measurements do not Necessarily identify the source of the problem, only that one exists.

4. Facilitate planning and control: productivity measurements provide information on Costs, time, output rate, and resource usage to allow decision making with respect to

pricing, production scheduling, purchasing, contracting, delivery scheduling, And many other activities in the industrial cycle. Productivity analysis, together with other elements of a competitive strategy, may determine which products or processes Should be expanded and which should be phased out.

5. Support innovation: productivity analysis, combined with cost data, aids in the evaluation of proposed changes to existing products or processes ones. It is one of the primary foundations for the continuous improvement effort that are both popular and necessary for survival in business firms today. The purpose of the measurement system is critically important in determining the specific measures to be used. For example, if the measures are to be used only for planning and control purposes, the inputs into the measures and the outputs may be imprecise, aggregate figures that provide guidance for setting schedules and future capacity requirements. If, however, the measures will be used as a basis for an employee evaluation system leading to bonuses, pay raises, layoffs, inputs and outputs of the measures must be more precise and accurate for shorter time period, and they must exclude factors outside the control of the worker. Questions of equity and interactions among individual jobs become evident.

The functions of monitoring performance and providing feedback, diagnosing problems, facilitating Planning and control, and supporting innovation are common to many types of measures, and Productivity is no exception. The function of defining productivity and directing behavior, however, warrants more explanation because it is important to managers in the successful operation of their Business units, and because it is important to researchers in the design of studies that shed light on Human behavior at work. In this obtique, we can come up with a simple of a waiter in a restaurant that Can be used to explain how measures of productivity can direct behavior. If the measure of productivity Is customers served per hour, the emphasis is on speed and throughout put, and the transaction as Quickly as possible. On the other hand, a measure of dollars of food served per customer would lead to Totally different behaviors; the waiter would suggest more expensive items and would encourage the Customer to have appetizers, wine, and dessert, regardless of the time taken. In this case, time is not A factor, the quick turnover of customers would be a disadvantage. Other possible measures could each lead to a different set of behaviors. One way to view individual productivity is to consider how the efforts of an individual Contribute to the productivity or success of the organization. Whether the actions of the waiter in each of the examples above would be productive depends on the Type of restaurant and specifically, its goals and objectives. A downtown Delicatessen would have one set of goals serving customers would be a distinct Advantage. A fine restaurant in the suburls would operate in a different milieu; Speed in this case could be a detriment. (Forrester, J. W. (1961).

The Fundamental question is not, what productivity measures should be used?

The fundamental question is, what are the organizational objectives? The Secondary question is, what set of individual productivity measures will direct The behavior of employees to meet those objectives as they work to ward their Own personal goals? The aim of the organization is to align work behavior with organizational goals. It is the responsibility of management, therefore, to develop measures that will elicit organizationally desirable behaviors. The requirement or ruling of effect, the cornerstone of operant psychology, says that behavior is a function of its consequences;; positive outcomes reinforce behaviors, which leads to their being repeated and expanded. Simply establishing a measure and feeding back the results to the employee can be regarded as a form of reinforcement; employees tend to work on the basis of the measure in any circumstances. If there is a net incentive for high performance, the link between behavior and the measure will be stronger. The greater the incentive, the stronger the relationship between the two. The term net incentive indicates that many incentives and disincentives may operate in a given set of circumstances.

For example:

- Organizational
- Goals
- Productivity
- Incentives
- Work
- Behavior

This figure is the goals, measurement, and behavior model. Peer pressure not to exceed production Standards, the desire by some for an easy job, and the tendency to socialize at work interact with Such positive incentives as financial rewards for high performance, opportunity for promotion, Satisfaction from a job well done, and many others. Worker motivation is a complex issue; in taking All of that complexity into consideration, the model suggests that the net incentive should be positive and tied to performance. Unfortunately, many organizational incentive systems are based on Productivity or other performance measures that are not in line with organizational goals. Programmers, for example, may be measured and rewarded for lines of code written per hour. Accountants may be evaluated on the number of reports produced, and maintenance personnel on the number of routine equipment overhauls performed. In each instance (and many more), maximization of the measured criterion would likely be counterproductive to the organization. Following the same logic, the productivity measurement system at each level of analysis should be Developed to direct behaviors and performance at one level of the organization to the goals at the Next higher level.

These relationships are depicted in their ideal state in my goal alignment model, figure 5-2.

Across the top of the method, the organization attempts to make business unit goals (at all intermediate levels) congruents with organization goals. Since the organization has no control over the individual goals or the non- work related goals of the group, it must accept them as given and design the organization to be compatible with them. For the sake of simplicity, this model does not consider Business:

- High level organizational Goals
- Individual measures Business unit organizational
- Group Measures
- Individual behavior business unit organizational
- Group behavior performance

Figure 5-2 Goal Alignment Model

The compatibility of individual goals affects performance, but it assumes that the behavior of one or the other, individual or group, is the basic unit of analysis determined by the process. Productivity Measures at the individual or group level direct behavior to the business unit goals, if properly aligned. That is, the individuals or groups will work to the measures; it's the responsibility of the organization to ensure that the measures are in line with the goals. Reading horizontally across the bottom of figure 5-2, the model indicates that the productivity (performance) of a business unit is a direct function of the Productive behavior of each of the individuals and groups within the unit. In turn, organizational Productivity of is a function of the productivity of each of the units. The degree to which this is true Depends on the definition of productivity at each level and the interactions among the elements Also, in this ideal model, the individual or group productivity results would sum to the productivity of the Next high business unit and ultimately to the productivity of the organization.

CHAPTER 4
HOW TO VALUE THE WORK
OF A GOOD WORKER
PERFORMANCE?

Giving evaluations can be difficult. Some workers react to criticism defensively. And, sometimes, no one understands what merits a positive evaluation. If your workers feel that you take it easy on some of them while coming down hard on others, resentment is inevitable. Avoid these problems by following these rules:

1. Be specific.

When you set goals and standards for your workers, spell out exactly what they will have to do to achieve them. For example, don't say "work harder "or "improve quality." Instead, say "increase sales by 20% over last year "or" make no more than three errors per day in data input." Similarly, when you evaluate a worker, give specific examples of what the employee did to achieve, or fall short of the goal.

2. Give Deadlines

If you want to see improvement, give the worker a timeline to turn things around. If you expect something to be done by a certain date, say so. (Hershauer, J. C. and W. A. Ruch. 91978).

3. Be Realistic

If you set unrealistic or impossible goals and standards, employers will have little Incentive to do their best if they know they will still fall short. Don't make your standards too easy to achieve but do take into account the realities of your workplace.

4. Be Honest

A common error in conducting performance analysis is over emphasizing the positive in order to avoid conflict or keep employees happy (a phenomenon called "leniency Error"). But this can lead to major problems for your company. If everyone gets the same positive performance recapitalization no matter what they do, employees will Have little incentive to do their best. Also, if you end up firing an employee for poor Performance, but the employee later claims he or she was fired for illegal reasons, you Won't have any documentation to back you up.

5. Be Complete

Write your evaluation so that an outsider reading it would be able to understand exactly What happened and why. Remember, that evaluation just might become evidence in a Lawsuit. If it does you will want the judge and jury to see why you rated the employee as you did.

6. Evaluate Performance, Not Personality

Target or focal point on how well (or poorly) the worker does the job, not on the worker's personal characteristics or traits for" instance, don't say the employee is "angry and emotional". Instead, target on the work-place conduct that is the problem for example, you can say the employee "has been insubordinate to managers twice in the past six months. This behavior is unacceptable and must stop".

7. Listen To Your Employees

The evaluation process will seem fairer to your workers if they have an opportunity to Express their concerns, too. Ask employees what they enjoy about their jobs and about Working at the company. Also ask about any concerns or problems they might have. You will gain valuable information, and your employees will feel like real participants in the process. In some cases, you might even learn something that could change your Evaluation. How do you value employees at work? In this manner, balancing work and Family is more important than salary for many workers. Employers value their Employees by acknowledging that their employees have priorities outside the workplace. Thus, giving employees greater flexibility is one way for companies to show they value employees' time and commitment.

HOW DO YOU MAKE SOMEONE FEEL VALUE AT WORK?

For example, you need:

1. Recognition
2. Feeback
3. Solicit their opinion and utilize it as often as possible
4. Communicate well, and frequently; keep them in the loop on what's happening at the organization.
5. Give direct compensation or benefit as a direct thank you, such as:
6. Give the benefits they want.

HOW TO MAKE EMPLOYEES FEEL APPRECIATED AND VALUED?

First of all, we have all heard the horror stories of those jobs where someone's Underappreciated and undervalued. When you are the boss, you don't want to be the cautionary tale. You need to make employees feel appreciated and valued and that their work's being noticed. We can notice that a meanwhile, ensuring them They are not in the cross hairs and ready to be replaced. As an employer, you have to ensure you make employees feel appreciated and valued in their workplace.

There are a lot of reasons for this. Most obviously, because it will make your employees enjoy coming to work, feel comfortable at work and allows them to produce their best work. By doing this, there are many things that can be done on behalf of the employer. Because at the end of the day, much of the aim is to create a culture that supports your employees. All the while giving the ability to produce great work. The best part about this is that it doesn't have to cost lots, it doesn't have to be timely. Really, all that's needed is good communication. After all, business is surely a relationship economy. At the end of the day this is what both you and your employee want. So, to help both of you meet these goals of great work and feeling valued, we have come up with six great tips to ensure your staff feel appreciated.

PLEASE, SPEND TIME WITH YOUR EMPLOYEES

It is nationally sure that employees can gain a great deal of satisfaction from a simple "thank you ", A bonus or pay rise. However, they feel valued the most when time is spent with the boss in a sum What less conventional way. For example, taking an employee out for lunch or out for a coffee can be More than enough to motivate them and make your employees feel appreciated. It can even be as easy as sitting down with them and discussing their thoughts on the job in depth. Or recapitulating their Performance in a personal manner and giving them some deserved feedback.

BE INTENTIONAL WITH EVERYDAY CONVERSATION. (Lawler, E. E., 9 1971)

A big part to make employees feel appreciated and in building relationships with your Team is through Effective and supportive communication. So, when you speak to employees, make sure they realize That they bring something to the company that nobody else can. It can be done in every day Conversations and can be an effective tool to build rapport.

HOW DO YOU EVALUATE STAFF PERFORMANCE?

The answer is that avoid these problems by following these rules:

1. Be Specific. When you set goals and standards for your workers, spell out exactly what they will have to do to achieve them.
2. Give deadlines
3. Be Realistic
4. Be Honest
5. Be Complete
6. Evaluate Performance, not Personality
7. Listen to Employees

HOW DO YOU MEASURE PERFORMANCE AT WORK?

Here are a few ways to measure and evaluate employee performance data:

1. Graphic rating scales a typical graphic scale uses sequential numbers, such as 1 to 5, or 1 to 10, to rate an employee's relative performance in specific areas.
2. 360 degrees feedback

3. Self-evaluation
4. Management by objectives (MBO).
5. Checklists

HOW EMPLOYEE PERFORMANCE IS MEASURED AND MANAGED?

Measuring and managing employee performance is the core of performance management, and it is a key to growing your business. Measuring employee job performance to continually improve skills and outcomes is a fundamental part of performance management Recapitulation process.

HOW DO YOU MEASURE PERFORMANACE GOALS?

Here are some guidelines that can help:

1. Establish goals in a face-to-face meeting. Work out a set goals for each employee.
2. Be sure the goals are measurable and written down.
3. State the goals in specific terms
4. Suit goals to the individual
5. Adjust goals that turn out to be unrealistic.

HOW DO YOU SET PERFORMANCE GOALS AT WORK?

Here are 10 things to keep in mind before setting goals at work and filing out that goal sheet:

1. Get Clarity on your Team's Structure

2. Talk to your Boss
3. Focus on what you can control and have a plan for the rest.
4. Think about your career path in the long run
5. Go beyond immediate and think of the big picture

A VALUED EMPLOYEE IS PREPARED FOR FAILURE

Although an employee who feels valued and a sense of worth in the work place will Be a successful worker overall, failure is always a part of a job. A valued employee Is prepared to take on a failure directly, learn from it, and more on. An employee That does not have that same sense of worth may feel devastated by even a more Minor flub, let alone a larger failure. (McGrath,J. E. (1984).

A VALUED EMPLOYEE CONNECTS AND INTERACTS

Many expects in the field of human resources have written extensively about how An employee with a bad attitude can quickly bring down the overall morale of a Work place. Conversely, an employee that feels a sense of value and worth on the Job is far more apt to connect and interact with his or her co-workers in a positive, Productive manner. Indeed, the presence of a valued worker and his/her positive Manifestations works to offset any negative energy being emanated or fostered by A worker who has a dim view of his/her situation.

HOW MANAGERS CAN SET PERFORMANCE GOALS FOR EMPLOYEES?

Setting goals for employees promotes engagement for associates and empowers managers to evaluate their individual Team members on measurable, viable facts, not just "feel" clearly defined goals increase the chance of success for both employees and their supervisors.

WHAT IMPACT DO GOALS HAVE ON SUCCESS?

By having realistic expectations, you motivate your employees to succeed. They understand exactly what they have to do to achieve the goal, and they believe That can do it. Having tangible goals like this increases motivation because people Can imagine themselves actually meeting your expectations.

WHAT IMPACT DO GOALS HAVE ON BEHAVIOR?

However, big or small, goals motivate everyone in virtually everything they do. A Goal may be as simple as "buy milk" or as complex as "develop a sustainable 10-year business plan." In either case, you know what you have to do. Setting goals for the employers at your small business changes their behavior, as well. A clear, attainable goal can light a fire under even the most aloof, unmotivated employees. You simply have to understand what aspect of the goal speaks to their needs and make it appeal to them.

REALISTIC EXPECTATIONS

You cannot set a goal that's too big or broad for your employees, as it only makes the task seem Unmanageable. By having realistic expectations, you motivate your employees to succeed. They Understand exactly what they must do to achieve their goal, and they believe that they can do it. Having tangible goals like this increases motivation because people can imagine themselves Meeting your expectations. If they feel confused by the goal or that the goal is unattainable, their Performance will suffer because they feel destined to disappoint.

SENSE OF PURPOSE

When employees have a goal, they have a sense of purpose that was otherwise missing. This increases Not only motivation and productivity but also morale. When employees feel like their actions are Actually making an impact in the company, they want to do well. Your employees don't want to feel like they don't make a difference or that they are simply a small piece of a big machine. When they have goals, they feel rewarded by their work and become more productive.

MEASURABLE PROGRESS

If you need to give your employees a big goal such as a six month or yearlong goal, make sure to break it up into smaller, easier pieces. For goals to influence behavior at all, they need to offer a measure of success as a way for their employees to see that they are doing well on a regular basis and that they are accomplishing everything they need. Goals motivate employees, but only if the deadlines are frequent enough to keep them working consistently. Goals that are too long term or offer no method of measuring progress may influence behavior negatively, encouraging people to put off their work until a later date. (Ruch, W. A., and J. C. Hershauer. (1974).

GOALS

Goals motivate people only if there is a reward involved. That isn't necessarily cynical, though. Remember that reward can be simple as getting credit for hard work. Whether your rewards are Monetary or not, promising them at the time of setting a goal motivates your employees to meet your Expectations. If your employees have goals without any sense that they will be compensated even with Just your appreciation their motivation will suffer.

GOALS OF EMPLOYEE PERFORMANCE EVALUATION

The goal of the best employee performance evaluation also include employee development and Organizational improvement. The goal of employee performance evaluation is to create accurate appraisal documentation to protect both the employee and the employer. The managers hate employee recapitulations because they don't like to sit in judgment about an Employee's work. They know that if the performance evaluation is less than settle they risk alienating The employee. At the same time, employee hate performance evaluation because they dislike being Judged. They tend to take suggestions for performance improvement personally and negatively. Performance management, on the other hand, provides the advantages organizations seek in doing Performance. The question on the table now is why organizations would want to ask employees to Participate in either employee performance evaluation or a performance management system. Good reasons exist for advocating the basic concept of performance evaluation. There are few fans of The traditional process.

WHERE EMPLOYEE PERFORMANCE EVALUATION FIT?

In some form, most organizations have an overall plan for business success. The employee Performance evaluation process, including goals setting, performance measurement, regular performance feedback, self-evaluation, employee recognition, and documentation of employee process., done with fit with care and understanding, helps employees see how their jobs and expected within the bigger picture of their organization.

The more effective evaluation processes accomplish these goals and have additional benefits. Documented performance evaluation are communication tools that ensure the supervisor, and her Reporting staff members are clear about the requirements of each employee's job. Evaluation. But Performance management participated effectively and with the appropriate mindset, accomplishes, Same goals, and more. Performance management also supplies additional advantages to both the manager and the employee. The employee performance evaluation provides evidence of non-discriminatory pay, and recognition processes. This is an important consideration consistent, regular, non- discriminatory employee performance evaluation. You want to ensure equitable measurement of an employee's contribution to the accomplishment of work, THE documentation of success and failure to achieve goals is a critical component of the employee performance evaluation systems take many forms organization to organization, these are the components that organizations are most likely to include Some are more effective than others. But the goals for the employee performance evaluation system, or the performance management process are similar. The differences appear in the approach and the details. And that can make all of the difference in how the performance evaluation system is perceived by and carried out by employees.

CHAPTER 5
PERFORMANCE MEASUREMENT
APPRAISAL OF WHAT
PERFORMANCE?

A corporate president put a senior executive in charge of a failing operation. His only directive was "Get it in the black." Within two years of that injunction, the new executive moved the operation from A deficit position to one that showed a profit of several Million. Fresh from his triumph, the executive Announced himself as a candidate for a higher-level position and indicated that he was already receiving offers from other companies. The corporate president, however, did not share the executive's position opinions of his behavior. In fact, the president, was not at all pleased with the way the executive had handled things. Generally, the executive was dismayed, and when he asked what he had done wrong, the corporate president told him that he had indeed accomplished what he had been asked to do, but he had done it single handedly, by the sheer force of his own personality. Additionally, the executive was told he had replaced people whom the company thought to be good employees with those it regarded as compliant. In effect, by demonstrating his own strength, he had made the organization weaker. Until the executive changed his authoritarian manner, his boss said, it was unlikely that he would be promoted further. Implicit in this scenario is the major fault in performance appraisal and management by objectives namely, a fundamental misconception of what is to be appraised. Performance appraisal has three basic functions L Abowd, J. (1990).

1. To provide adequate feedback to each person on his or her performance;
2. To serve as a basis for Modifying or changing behavior toward more effective working habits; and
3. To provide data to Managers with they may judge future job assignments and compensation

The performance appraisal Concept is central to effective management. Much hard and imaginative work has gone into developing and refining it. In fact, there is a great deal of evidence to indicate how useful and effective Performance appraisal is. Yet present systems of performance appraisal do not serve any of these Functions well. As it is customarily defined and used, performance appraisal focuses not on behavior but on outcomes of behavior. But even though the executive in the example achieved his objective, He was evaluated on how he attained it. Thus, while the system purports to appraise result, in practice, people are really appraised on how they do things, which is not formally described in the setting of objectives, and for which there are rarely data on record. In my experience, the crucial aspect of any manager's job and the source of most failures, which is practically never described, is the "how ". As long as managers appraise the e yet actually give greater weight to the means, employ a state job description base which does not describe the how ", and do not have support mechanisms for the appraisal process, widespread dissatisfaction with performance appraisal is bound to continue. In fact, one personnel authority speaks of performance appraisal as "the Achilles heel of our profession". Just how these inadequacies affect performance appraisal systems and how they can be corrected to Provide managers with realistic bases for making judgments about employee's performance is the Subject of this article. (Adams, J. (1965).

INADEQUACIES OF APPRAISAL SYSTEMS

It is widely recognized that there are many things inherently wrong with most of the performance Appraisal systems in use.

The most obvious drawbacks are:

1. No matter how well defined the Dimensions for appraising performance on quantitative goals are, judgments on performance are Usually subjective and impressionistic. Because appraisals provide inadequate information about the Subtleties of performance, managers using them to compare employees for the purposes of Determining salary increases often make arbitrary judgments. Ratings by different managers, and especially those in different units, are usually incomparable. What is excellent work in one unit may Be unacceptable in another in the same company. (Allan, P., and Rosenberg, S. (1986).

2. When salary Increases are allocated on the basis of curve of normal distribution, which is in turn based on rating of Results rather them on behavior, competent employees may not only be denied increases but may also become demotivated.

3. Trying to base promotion and layoff decisions on appraisal data leaves the decisions open to acrimonious debate. When employees who have retired early have complained to federal authorities of age discrimination, defendant companies have discovered that there was inadequate data to support the layoff decisions.

4. Although managers are urged to give feedback freely and often, there are no built-in mechanisms for ensuring that they do so. Delay in feedback creates both frustrations, when good performance is not quickly recognized and anger, when judgment is rendered for inadequacies long past. (Allison, G. (1983).

5. There are few effective established mechanisms to cope with either the sense of inadequacy managers has about appraising subordinates, or the paralysis and procrastination that result from guilt about playing some people might argue that these problems are deficiencies of managers, not of the system. But even if that were altogether true managers are part of that system. Performance appraisal needs to be viewed not as a technique but as a process involving both people and data, and as such the whole process is inadequate.

Recognizing that there are many deficiencies in performance appraisal, managers in many companies Do not want to do them. In order companies there is a great reluctance to do them straight forwardly. Forms in use in many companies to day have such directions as:

1. "List the major objectives of this Person's job that can be measured qualitatively or quantitatively".

2. "Define the results expected and the standards of performance money, quantity, time limits, or completion dates".

3. "Describe the Action planned as a result of this appraisal, the next steps to be taken, reevaluation, strategy, tactic, And so on.

4. "List the person's strong point, his assets and accomplishments and his weak point areas in which improvement is needed. What are the action plans for improvement? In most instances the Appraiser is asked to do an overall rating with a five-point scale or some similar device. Finally, he is Asked to make a statement about the person's potential for the next step or even for higher level Management. No where in this set of questions or in any of the performance appraisal systems I have Examined is anything asked about how the person is to attain the ends he or she is charged with reaching. With some may asset that the ideal way of managing is to give a person a charge and leave him or her alone to accomplish it, this principle is over simplified

both in theory and practice. People need to know the two photographs of the land they are expected to cross, and the routes as perceived by those to whom they report.

CHAPTER 6
LEADERSHIP SKILLS AND THE
VALUES OF AN ORGANIZATION

Explain how Leaders have an outstanding impact on organizational culture?

It is understood that Leaders have an outstanding impact on organizational culture. Employees tend to Follow leaders in professional and culture ways leading to a broad impact on the organization as a whole. Leadership is commonly defined as establishing a clear vision, communication and resolving the immediate conflicts among the employees or facing the organization as a whole. Leaders are tasked with efficiently guiding organizational goal achievement while considering Team member skills essential to produce the desired productivity. (Allport, G.W.(1961). Since leadership is an aspect of management, it is necessary to establish that the management is well-equipped with leadership skills.

Effective leadership can influence the organizational values such as honesty, respect, ethics and tolerance etc. by demonstrating an ideal attitude in the workplace, establishing a vision among the employees, reinforcing accountability, motivating the employees, making a vision plan for the culture and values and by coaching the co-workers.

1. IDEAL BEHAVIOR AND ATTITUDE

The management can present professional yet friendly attitude in the work-place. Change can Only be expected by employees when management implement it first. According to the trait Theory of leadership, one must be well-equipped with a certain set of personal qualities and Characteristics such as intelligence, good judgment, decisiveness etc. for the people to follow Him. In order to reinforce this behavior, it must be awarded and appreciated when acted upon.

The law of effect and reinforcement theory can be utilized, which says that a favorable after-Effect strengthens the action that produced it. This means that actions followed by satisfaction Will become firmly attached to the situation and therefore are more likely to occur. Establishing purpose, vision, and goals among the employees. People always need a purpose to believe in and need to know what is most expected of them. Communication with employees is a key on the organization's purpose, the image that needs To be maintained and the amount of productivity that is required of them can bring a huge Impact on the perspective of organization values among the employees. This may not only increase productivity but also give a chance to emotionally connect with all the co-workers.

2. ESTABLISHING A CULTURE OF ACCOUNTABILITY

Accountability is one of the keyways for leaders to influence the culture of the organization. This Begins with having detailed job descriptions and clearly establishing measures and goals. Further Communicating the HR manual and policies of the organization to employees and making them Compulsory to read will be another major step. The employees need to see that all the internal Processes, controls and systems, and culture elements are in place for a reason. Further taking Necessary actions in case of discrepancies and other fall- outs will be necessary to bring order and Eliminate conflicts within the organizational culture. (Baker, S. (1996).

3. MOTIVATION AND INTEREST

This involves having a personal connection with your co-workers in order to understand what drives Them. Using Maslow's hierarchy of needs, by assessing the interest of the employees critically, Positive change can be inscribed within the organization. Further according to Herzberg theory, the hygiene (factors causing dissatisfaction) and motivator factors (factors causing satisfaction) For the employees can be studied through survey or communication. after studying these with Proper leadership skills applied, values of the organization can be instilled among these co-workers. This can be done through friendly interpersonal communication, seminars, formal dinners and training.

4. DEVISING THE VISION PLAY OF ORGANIZATIONAL VALUES

Vision is the foundation for goal achievement within the organization. Awareness of the organizational Vision provides a directional compass for each contributor within the organization to follow in terms of Efficiency and work environment. Effective leadership is responsible for articulating the vision. Speaking more about the value of the work and the company and not compromising on quality and Ethics can bring the right impact within the organization. Moreover, aligning the employees to work as a team to operational strategies by making them realize their importance. This can be done by involving them in brainstorming sessions, inquiring with them for feedback and suggestions. This can help employees feel confident and important within the organization. Therefore, reassuring them that their actions will have an impact on the organization itself. These steps taken by effective leadership are necessary to achieve company priorities by maintaining organizational values in connection with the vision of the organization. (Beck, D.E. and Cowan, C.C. (1996).

5. COACHING THE CULTURE CLUB

Leader coaching and development provides the framework for the employees to contribute to the company strategy and achievement of goals while maintaining the company values. Organizational values can be instructed by effective leadership. These values may be accountability, focusing on details, making a difference, delivering quality, healthy work-place environment, Honesty, reliability and positivity, helping others, meeting deadlines, respecting company policy and rules and showing tolerance and respect among each other. Leadership can therefore Immensely influence the values of an organization provided the leaders are well-equipped with Professional and leadership qualities.

HOW COULD LEADERSHIP PERSONALITY TRAITS RELATE TO EFFECTIVE LEADERSHIP?

At work, leader's personal traits can affect critical organizational success factors as motivation ,Performance, dealing with presentations.

HOW THE PERSONALITY OF LEADERS INFLUENCE LEADERSHIP BEHAVIOR?

The personality of leaders has a significant influence on the way they sense, think, believe and communicate with other people. Leader's personality influences their behavior, controls their attitudes, and affects the way they Perceive about things. Both perception and attitude play an imperative function in forming leadership behavior. Different people have different personal traits. So, inevitably, they act differently in different situations. A leader's interpersonal skills have a direct impact on the way they act and react to different work situations. At work, a leader's personal traits can affect critical organizational success factors such as motivation, performance, and effectiveness. Leaders who have extravert personality trait are seen to be good at organizing effective meetings and dealing with presentations. Leaders who have less agreeableness often take more time to be skilled at team building, directing and mentoring. Leaders who have positive personal traits such as openness and agreeableness are good at managing larger teams and mediating conflicts among team members. Leaders, who have candidness and high emotional stability, are usually capable of driving a positive attitude towards his or her work responsibilities. Leaders who have self-efficacy and conscientiousness are capable to making effective decisions even when they are under severe pressure. A good leader must have to be to understand his personality and figure out how his personality traits influence his behavior at the workplace. The more leaders can understand their personality, the better they are able to identify their negative personality traits. Though cognitive personality traits are often very difficult to change, non- cognitive personality traits are often seen to be improvable. Moreover, most individuals have a more-less capability of adapting their personal styles in accordance with a specific situation. Therefore, leaders need to study their personality traits and learn how they can improve it to positively influence their work-place behavior. (Bilsky, W. & Schwartz, E.H. (1994).

HOW COULD LEADERSHIP PERSONALITY TRAITS RELATE TO EFFECTIVE LEADERSHIP?

At work, leader's personal traits can affect critical organizational success factors such as motivation, Performance, and effectiveness. Leaders who have extravert personality trait are seen to be good at organizing effective meetings and dealing with presentations.

WHAT IS THE ROLE OF LEADER IN SHAPING AND REINFORCING CULTURE?

However, the leader's behavior sets the tone for the organization. Leader's values, actions, and the Development of their Teams need to visibly reinforce the culture of the organization. Through the Example they set, leaders shape the culture in their words and actions every day.

HOW DOES LEADERSHIP INFLUENCE CULTURE?

Leaders have a powerful influence on an organization's culture. They set the tone for how employees Perceive their work experience, so leadership and culture go hand in hand. Besides nurturing those qualities, there are some specific things you can do to improve your impact on company culture.

WHAT ROLE DOES LEADRERSHIP PLAY IN INFLUENCING ORGANIZATIONAL BEHAVIOR?

Leadership is the action of leading people in an organization towards achieving goals. Leaders do this by influencing employee behaviors in several ways. A leader sets a clear vision for the organization, (Finkelstein, S and Hambrick, D.(1996). Motivates employees, guides employees through the work Process and builds morale.

WHY IS CULTURE IMPORTANT IN LEADERSHIP?

An essential skill for successful superintendents is culture leadership. Culture is important because it can powerfully influence human behavior.

WHY IS CULTURE LEADERSHIP IMPORTANT TO A 21st CENTURY?

Culture is important because it can powerfully influence human behavior. Culture is powerful because:

1. Individuals are selected and indoctrinated so well;
2. The culture exerts itself through the Actions of a large number of people; and
3. All of this happens without much conscious intent making it difficult to challenge or at even to discuss (Kotter, 1996)

It is crucial for superintendents to understand the power of culture on the organization and that culture trumps everything. Leadership is critical. Leaders create and reinforce norms and behaviors that are expected within The culture. What leaders stress as important, how they confront crises, what they role-model, and Who they bring in and allow to remain in the organization are powerful in establishing norms for a Culture. Superintendent effectiveness is dependent upon one's skills in cultural leadership. (Deal, T.E. And Peterson, K.D. (1999).

CHAPTER 7
THE ROLE OF LEADERSHIP IN EMPLOYEE MOTIVATION

First of all, every organization, like every Team, requires leadership. Leadership allows managers to Affect employee behavior in the organization. Thus, motivated employees are one of the most Important results of effective leadership. According to (Abbas & Asgar 2010-9), successful managers Are successful leaders because they influence employees to help accomplish organizational goals. Achieving organizational goals, however, is not enough to keep employees motivated but helping Employees accomplish their own personal and career goals is an important part of their motivation. Leadership and motivation are interactive. Leadership effectiveness is critically contingent on, and Often defined in terms of leaders 'ability to motivate followers toward collective goals or a collective Mission or vision (Shamir, Zakay, Breinin, & Popper 1998:390).The more motivated the supporters, The more effective the leader; the more effective the leader, the more motivated the followers. Leadership is a: social influence process that is necessary for the attainment of societal and organization Goals; it is both conspicuous in its absence and mysterious in its presence, familiar and yet hard to" (Faeth 2010:2). Leaders understand that they have power and that they understand the source of their Power: their position; their ability to reward and to coerce; their expertise; and their personal appeal and charisma. They influence their followers' behavior through communication, group dynamics, Training, rewards and discipline. There are many types of leadership types, namely: transformational, Situational, autocratic, visionary and charismatic leadership. While this study is to draw from the Autocratic and transformational leadership styles to advance further understanding on the underlying Mechanisms that enable leaders to behave in an autocratic or transformational manner, and to affect Employee motivation, their behavior and consequently, their organizational oriented ventures. The Insubstantial intends to establish the role of leadership style in motivating the teaching staff to be Committed to their work. (Allert, J.& Chatterjee, S. (1997)

LEADERSHIP

Leadership is complex because it is studied in different ways that entail different definitions. In this Case, it can be defined as the process of a leader communicating ideas, gaining acceptance of the vision and motivating followers to support and implement the ideas through others (Lussier 2013). A leader Always has the ability to influence others and may not necessary be a manager, whereas another Person can possess leadership qualities and also be a manager. There are three types of managerial Leadership skills, namely: Technical skills, interpersonal skills and Decision-Making skills. Technical Skills are ideally concerned with the ability to use methods and techniques to perform a task; Interpersonal skills, on the other hand, focus solely on the ability to understand, communicate and Work well with individuals and groups through developing effective relationships. Finally, decision-making skills involve the ability to conceptualize situations and select alternatives to solve problems and take advantage of opportunities (Faith 2010).

TRANSFORMATIONAL AND AUTOCRATIC LEADERSHIP STYLES

What transformational and autocratic leadership style's role?

Transformational leadership seeks to change the status quo by articulating to followers, problems in The current system and a compelling vision of what a new organization could be (Lussier 2013).Transformational leaders are often known for moving and changing things in major ways by Communicating to followers a clear vision of the future by tapping into followers' highest ideals and motives. They are said to be powerful in transforming a weak or declining organization by influencing followers/employees to be convinced by their new vision, ideas and possibilities. They effect positive change in organizational culture and learning. Transformational leadership behaviors include, among other things, four major components: inspirational motivation; idealized influence; individualized consideration; and intellectual stimulation (Bass & Avolio 1994). Kirk and Dijk (2007) further explain that inspirational motivation includes the creation and presentation of an attractive vision of the future; the use of symbols and emotional arguments; and the demonstration of optimism and enthusiasm. Idealized influence includes such behaviors as: sacrificing for the benefit of the group; setting a personal example; and demonstrating high ethical standards. Individualized consideration Includes providing support, encouragement, and coaching to followers. Finally, intellectual stimulation Involves behaviors that increase an awareness of problems and challenge followers to view problems From new perspectives.

MOTIVATION

Motivation is the driving force in pursuing and satisfying one's needs (Kontodimopoulos, Paleologou & Niakas 2009). It is anything that affects behavior in pursuing a certain outcome. (Appelbaum, C & Hebert, D. and Leroux, L. (1999). Motivation is also defined as the process that accounts for an Individual 's passion, direction, and persistence of effort toward attaining a goal, meaning the result of the interaction between an individual and a situation (Robbins, Judge, Odendaal Roodt 2009). Motivation focuses on an includes the processes that guide the general strength and direction of a Person's action over time. This duration is of great important because although motivated behavior Takes place only in the present, its direction is toward the future 9 Bernard, Mills, Swenson & Wash 2005). Motivation is a fundamental instrument for regular work behavior of employees (Olusola 2011). The motivation to work, whether intrinsic or extrinsic, is critical in the lives of employees because it forms the essential reason for working in life (O lolube 2006). Intrinsic motivation is regulated by personal enjoyment, interest or pleasure (Lai 2011) and it involves the performance of an activity for the inherent satisfaction of an activity. Extrinsic motivation refers to doing something because it is inherently stimulating or enjoyable (Ryan & Ded 2000).

LEADERSHIP & MOTIVATION

The success of every organization depends on its employees' drive to thrive through their efforts, Commitment, engagement, practice and persistence. Thus, motivation is an important topic because Leadership competencies include the ability to motivate employees (Lussier 2013) as one of the crucial Duties or jobs. Leadership begins with the initial effort made to recruit a new employee; proceeds Through the entire induction process; and continues every day until the employee departs the organization. This process is cultivated by a manager/ leader. motivating new employees and it highlights, once again, the importance of leadership to an organization. (Aaltio-Marjosala I. & Lehtimen J. (1998). The quality of a manager's relationship with an employee is the most powerful Element of employee motivation. It creates a professional, positive and respectful attitude and Employees are more likely to adopt a similar approach with their peers and enjoy work. It is clear that the management and leadership styles that are adopted by a business and its management Will have a determining effect on the motivation level, the morale and the job satisfaction of the

Employees. Nevertheless, the relationship between the management style that is used within the Business and the level of motivation within the workforce is a subject of much debate within industry. In many circles there is continuous debate about whether leaders are born or developed. Reflecting on the discussions about motivation, it is evident that humans are very complicated and are made up of a Number of traits. With motivation, these influences are both inherited and acquired from our Environment and influences (Gary 1996). It is in this regard that the study seeks to establish the role of leadership on employee motivation.

EVALUATION OF CONCEPTUAL WEAKNESS IN TRANSFORMATIONAL AND CHARISMATIC LEADERSHIP THEORIES

The conceptual weakness in transformational leadership theory is examined first, followed by an Examination of conceptual weaknesses in charismatic leadership theory. The conceptual weaknesses I found are similar to those in most earlier leadership theories, and they include ambiguous constructs, Insufficient description of explanatory processes, a narrow focus on dyadic processes, omission of Some relevant behaviors, sufficient specification of limiting conditions (situational variables), and a bias toward heroic conceptions of leadership. Then I discuss the issue of compatibility between transformational and charismatic leadership. The final section provides a summary and conclusions. Throughout the project I make suggestions for improving the theories and point out additional research That is needed to evaluate them. Altio-Marjosola,I.& Takala,T. (2000).

TRANSFORMATIONAL LEADERSHIP

The version of transformational leadership theory that has generated the most research was formulated By Bass and his colleagues Bass 1985, Bass 1996. They define transformational leadership primarily in Terms of the leader's effect on followers, and the behavior used to achieve this effect. The followers Feel trust, admiration, loyalty, and respect toward the leader, and they are motivated to do more than They originally expected to do. The underlying influence process is described in terms of motivating Followers by making them more aware of the importance of task outcomes and inducing them to Transcend their own self-interest for the sake of the organization. Transformational leadership is Differentiated from transactional leadership, which involves an exchange process to motivate follower Compliance with leader requests and organizational rules. Most factor studies support the proposed distinction between transformational and transactional behavior (Bass, 1996), but a number of discrepancies have been found. Some studies find that positive reward behavior depends on the transformational factor instead of the transactional factor. Other studies find that laissez-faire leadership and passive management by exception form a separate factor rather than loading on transactional leadership Den Hartog, Van Muijen, & Koopman 1997, Lievens, Van Geit, & Coetsier 1997, Yammarino& Bass 1990. Since the theory deals primarily with dyadic processes, it is not Surprising that there is better coverage of transformational behaviors at the dyadic level than at the group and organizational levels. Inspiring and developing are well represented in the MLQ. However, important empowering behaviors such as consulting, delegating, and sharing of sensitive information are not directly represented in the MLQ. Bass (1996) has contended that transformational and transactional leadership can be either directive (autocratic) or participative, but this is a weak argument for excluding behaviors that seem so directly relevant to the influence processes underlying transformational leadership. Participation and delegation involve internalization when feeling s of ownership for a decision link it more closely to a follower's self-concept and self-work. Although no single theory should be expected to include all aspects of leadership behavior, use of the label' full range leadership theory" by Bass (1996) invites critical evaluation of completeness. A full range theory should include not only the missing transformational behaviors mentioned earlier but also types of behavior that are not part of either transformational or transactional leadership. One obvious omission is task-oriented behavior relevant for effective leadership (e.g., clarifying expected results, setting specific task goals, operational planning, coordinating activities, allocating resources, monitoring operations in a non-obtrusive way). Another omission involves leader interaction with superiors, peers, and outsiders whose information, cooperation and political support are essential for a group's performance of its mission (e.g., networking, acting as spokesperson for the group, negotiating agreements, persuading people to provide political support and necessary resources, resolving problems and conflicts with outsiders. The search for situational moderator variables may be more successful if directed at specific types of transformational behavior. Even if there is always some type of transformational behavior that is relevant for effective leadership, not every type of transformational behavior will be relevant in every situation. Because of the high inter-correlation among transformational leadership scales in the MLQ, the survey studies have not been useful for assessing the separate effects of these component behaviors. The descriptive studies on transformational leadership also fail to provide a good basis for assessing facilitating or limiting conditions. To identify situational moderator effects, more accurate measures of leader behavior should be used (e.g., observations, diaries) instead of relying so much on behavior questionnaires. This research should include independent sources of information about leader behavior, mediating variables, outcome variables, and situational variables. More field experiments are also needed to assess the causal effects of mediating and situational variables. Laboratory experiments (e.g., Kirkpatrick & Locke, 1996) may also be useful. However, to ensure that the key influence processes in transformational leadership actually occur, it Is desirable to have a simulation that extend over several weeks and involves a meaningful task.

WHAT DO YOU THINK ABOUT THE INSUFFICIENT IDENTIFICATION OF NEGATIVE EFFECTS?

Naturally, the theory does not explicitly identify any situation where transformational leadership Is detrimental. However, the possibility that transformational leadership can have negative outcomes Methods designed to detect such effects.

NOW LET US TALK ABOUT HEROIC LEADERSHIP BIAS

The Heroic Leadership Bias is like most earlier leadership theories, and the transformational Leadership theories reflect the implicit assumptions associated with the 'heroic leadership "stereotype Calder 1977, Meind Ehrlich, & Dukerich 1985. Effective performance by an individual, group, or Organization is assumed to depend on leadership by an individual with the skills to find the right path and motivate others to take it. In most versions of transformational leadership theory, it is a basic Postulate that an effective leader will influence followers to make self- sacrifices and exert exceptional effort. Influence is unidirectional, and it flows from the leader to the follower. When a correlation is found between transformational leadership and subordinate commitment or performance, the results are interpreted as showing that the leader influenced subordinate to perform better. There is little interest in describing reciprocal influence processes or shared leadership. Researchers study how leaders motivate followers or overcome their resistance, not how leaders encourage followers to challenge the leader's vision or develop a better one. (Bass B.M. (1985). An alternative perspective would be to describe leadership as a shared process of enhancing the collective and individual capacity of people to accomplish their work roles effectively. This alternative conception of leadership does not require an individual who can perform all of the essential leadership functions, only a set of people who collectively perform them. Some leadership functions (e.g., making important decisions) may be shared by several members of a group, some leadership functions may be allocated to individual members, and a particular leadership function may be performed by different people at different times. (Bensman J. 7 Givant M. (1975).

The leadership actions of any individual leader are much less important than the collective leadership by the members of the organization. The transformational leadership theory by Burns (1978) Seems to Take this perspective more than the others, but all of the theories would be improved by a more explicit description of the implications for distributed and shared leadership in groups and organizations.

TELL US ABOUT THE CHARISMATIC LEADERSHIP?

Charismatic leadership is the original charismatic leadership theory by Weber (1947) described how Followers attribute extraordinary qualities (charisma) to the leader. In recent years, others have Modified and extended this theory to describe charismatic leadership in formal organizations (Conger,1989; Conger & Kanungo, 1988, Conger 7 Kanungo 1998, House 1977; Shamir and associates 1993).

These theories describe charismatic leadership in terms of the amount of leader influence over followers and the type of leader-follower relationship that emerges. The core behaviors in charismatic leadership Vary somewhat from theory to theory, and sometimes from older to newer versions of the same theory. The key behaviors in the Conger and Kanungo (1988, 1998) theory include articulate an innovation strategic vision, showing sensitivity to member needs, displaying unconventional behavior, taking personal risks, and showing sensitivity to the environment (identifying constraints, threats, And opportunities. The key behaviors in the House (1977) and Shamir et al. (1993) theories include Articulating an appealing vision, emphasizing ideological self-confidence, modeling, exemplary behavior, and emphasizing collective identity. Some researchers have further differentiated between the content of the vision and the use of an expressive style to communicate it (e.g., Kirl Patrick & Locke, 1996). There is need for more clarity and consistency in how the term charismatic is defined and used. The most useful definition seems to be in terms of attributions of charisma to a leader by followers who Identify strongly with the leader. This definition maintains the original meaning of charisma and provides a basis for differentiating between charismatic and transformational leadership. (Blum, Lawrence A. (1998).

AMBIGUITY ABOUT UNDERLYING INFLUENCE PROCESSES.

The theorists also disagree about the relative importance of the underlying influence processes. Personal identification was the primary influence process in the initial version of the charismatic Leadership theory proposed by Conger and Kanungo (1987). In their most recent version of the theory (Conger & Kanungo, 1998), personal identification is the primary process early in the relationship, but Internalization becomes more important later in the relationship. The theory by Shamir and associates (1993) appears to emphasize internalization and collective identification more than personal Identification. Which influence process is dominant may be very relevant for understanding leadership Effectiveness Howell 1988, Kelman 1974, Shamir 1991.When there is strong personal identification, Followers are passionately devoted to an attractive leader with exceptional ability to find solutions to Important problems confronting them. Followers desire to be like the leader and to gain the leader's Acceptance and approval. They will imitate the leader's behavior, accept the leader's task objectives, comply with the leader's requests, and make self-sacrifices and an extra effort in the work to please the Leader. In extreme cases, the follower's primary self-identify may become service to the leader. Strong Personal identification creates loyal, obedient followers, but it may inhibit them from providing feedback to the leader or showing initiative. They will be reluctant to disagree with the leader, criticize the leader's plans, or deviate from them. They will tend to ignore or rationalize any evidence that the plans and policies proposed by their leader are unrealistic and impractical. A somewhat different type of relationship seems likely when the primary influence process is internalization, and task objectives are linked to a follower's core values and self-identity. When followers come to see their work roles as an important part of their self-identity, successful performance becomes very impo9rtant for their self-acceptance and self-worth. Followers will make self-sacrifices and exert extra effort in their work to facilitate achievement of the task objectives. In extreme cases, service to the cause may become a follower's primary self-identity. The dedication of subordinates to the mission will be stronger than any loyalty they feel to the leader. Followers are likely to express concerns about leader plans and policies that appear to be impractical or self-serving, and they may refuse to carry out a request that appears to endanger the mission or violate their core values. The charismatic leadership theories would improve by a better explanation of the underlying influence processes. (Bryman A. (1992). How do personal identification, social identification, internalization, and instrumental compliance interact in determining the behavior of followers? Is one influence process more central than the others? How are these influence processes related to leader influence processes in charismatic leadership, and it remains the most speculative aspect of the theories. Leadership by executives has increased over the past decade (see Finkelstein & Hambrick 1996, Schein 19992, Trice & Beyer 1993, Zaccaro 1996), but as yet it has Not been integrated very well with the dominant theories of charismatic leadership.

AMBIGUITY ABOUT ESSENTIAL BEHAVIORS

Differences among the theories with regard to the essential behaviors in charismatic leadership have Created some ambiguity that should be resolved. The set of behaviors in the most recent version of the Conger and Kanungo (1998) theory is consistent with their initial theory and findings in their early research comparing charismatic to non-charismatic leaders (Conger & Kanunger, 1988). The theory proposed by Shamir and associates (1993) includes not only the initial set of behaviors proposed by House (1977), but also some behaviors borrowed from other charismatic and transformational theories. The link between behaviors and explanatory processes is not always clear, and some of the behaviors appear to have been selected because they are relevant to leadership effectiveness rather than because they increase attributions of charisma. Some behaviors that appear relevant for understanding charismatic leadership were overlooked in the theories and the related research. There seems to be a preference for socially acceptable behaviors rather than manipulative behaviors that increase followers' perception of leader expertise and dependence on the leader. Some examples of these manipulative behaviors are the following: misinterpreting events or inciting incidents to create the appearance of miracles; using staged events with music and symbols to arouse emotions and build enthusiasm; covering up mistakes and failures; blaming others for the leader's mistakes; (Burrel, G& Morgan. K (1979). Limiting member access to information about operations and performance; limiting the scope of subordinate work roles; limiting communication of criticism or dissent; indoctrinating new members; using deference rituals and status symbols; and creating barriers to isolate members from contacts with outsiders.

INSUFFICIENT SPECIFICATION OF FACILITATING CONDITIONS

There is still ambiguity about the necessary conditions for attributions of charisma. The essential Characteristics of the leader have been discussed extensively, but the essential characteristics of Followers have received less attention. The theories suggest that followers are more susceptible if they are insecure, alienated, fearful about their physical safety or economic security, they lack self-esteem, and they have a weak self-identity. As yet there has been little empirical research to verify that such Followers are more prone to attributions of charisma and strong personal identification with a leader. More effort should be made to identify relevant follower characteristics and explain how they are Related to leader characteristics, underlying influence processes, and contextual variables. (Conger, J. and Kanungo, R. (1996). One contextual variable that has been of special interest is the existence Of a crisis. In Weber's (1947) theory a crisis was necessary for the emergence of a charismatic leader. One contextual variable that has been of special interest is the existence of a crisis. In Weber's (1947) Theory a crisis was necessary for the emergence of a charismatic leader. In the more recent theories (Conger and Kanungo, 1988, Conger & Kanungo 1998, Shamir et al. 1993), a crisis facilitates charismatic leadership but is not a necessary antecedent condition. In the absence of a real crisis, the Leader may be able to interpret events in a way that exaggerates environmental threats, or the leader may covertly precipitate incidents that make a crisis seem more imminent (Boal & Bryson, 1988). Another alternative is the possibility that a leader can identify opportunities for significant innovations That will greatly benefit followers (Conger & Kanungo, 1998). For example, the CEO of a successful Company initiates a joint venture, or a clever entrepreneur founds an organization to provide a new Type of product or service. An uncertain, turbulent environment is probably a facilitating condition for charismatic leadership, because turbulence increases both the threats and opportunities for an organization. An interesting research question is whether the same behaviors and influence processes Are associated with charismatic leadership in crisis and non-crisis situations.

AMBIGUITY ABOUT REASONS FOR LOSS OF CHARISMA

Charisma is transitory: It can be gained or lost as conditions change Bryman 1992, Roberts &Bradley 1988. Charismatic leadership theory needs a more detailed explanation of how charisma is lost by a leader. It is clear to what extent the same conditions that facilitate the acquisition of charisma are also involved in its loss. (Gardner W. & Avolio B. (1998). It seems likely that attributions of charisma to the leader will diminish if the antecedent crisis ends, or if followers become more confident and capable of solving problems for themselves. Other possible reasons for loss of charisma include leader decisions that result in obvious failure, leader betrayal of followers, and the appearance of rivals who are even more attractive and credible than the leader.

TRANSFORMATIONAL VERSUS CHARISMATIC LEADERSHIP

The one of the most important conceptual issues for transformational and charismatic leadership is the extent to which they are similar and compatible. Some theorists minimize the drenches between Transformational and charismatic leadership (e.g., House &

Shamir, 1993). It is now common practice in many books and articles to treat the two approaches as equivalent. The assumption of equivalence Has been challenged by leadership scholars (myself include) Who view transformational and charismatic leadership as distinct but partially overlapping processes. (Geertz C. (1983). Proposed that charisma is a necessary component of transformational leadership, but he noted that a leader can be charismatic without being transformational. Several writers have proposed that a leader can be transformational without being charismatic. A few writers have even suggested the possibility that the two types of leadership may be incompatible (Yukl, 1994). Conceptual ambiguity and a lack of consistency in the use of terms make it difficult to compare transformational leadership to charismatic leadership. How much similarity one finds depends on which versions of the theories are compared. In recent years, the major charismatic theories have been revised to incorporate additional forms of Effective leadership behavior. The term "Transformational" has been broadly defined by many writers to include almost any type of effective leadership, regardless of the underlying influence processes. The label may refer to the transformational of individual followers or to the transformational of entire Organizations. If the two types of leadership are essentially similar, they can be integrated into a single Theory. Similarity also means that it is justifiable to cite results from studies testing one theory as Evidence for the other, which has become a common practice in leadership literature. The amount of similarity between charismatic and transformational leadership is both a conceptual and empirical Question. There is little reason for making a distinction between the two types of leadership unless they Are defined in a way that involves important differences in underlying processes, and these differences can be verified by empirical research. The research should determine not only whether transformational and charismatic leadership can occur simultaneously in the same individual, but also whether this combination is common or rare, and whether it is stable or unstable over time. I propose that the simultaneous occurrence of transformational and charismatic leadership is both uncommon and unstable. There is little reason to expect that the core behaviors in transformational leadership will automatically result in attributed charisma. In fact, the developing and empowering behaviors associated with transformational leadership seem to make it less likely that followers will developing and empowering behaviors associated with transformational leadership seem to make it less likely that followers will attribute extraordinary qualities to the leader. (Geertz C. (1983). It is important to recognize that the existing research does not provide a definitive answer about the compatibility of transformational and charismatic leadership. Neither the survey studies nor the descriptive studies were designed to investigate this research question. The utility of the survey research is greatly reduced by the high multicollinearity among the behavior scales and the low level of measurement accuracy. The biographies and descriptive accounts seldom provide a complete and objective examination of the Relevant variables. To find an answer to this important research question may require intensive, Longitudinal research that measures not only leader characteristics, but also influence processes, Follower characteristics and relevant aspects of the situation. To conclude and summarize, it is evident that charismatic and transformational leadership theories provide important insights, but some serious conceptual weaknesses need to be corrected to make the theories more useful. They do Not describe the underlying influence processes clearly, nor do they specify how the leader behaviors Are related to these processes. It seems that instrumental compliance is most important for transactional leadership, internalization is most important for transformational leadership, and personal identification is most important for charismatic leadership. However, the relevance of these and other influence processes. They are difficult to study, but they hold great promise for improving our understanding of effective leadership. There is also considerable ambiguity about the essential behaviors for charismatic and transformational Leadership. Many of the same behaviors appear relevant for both types of leadership, but there are Some apparent differences in the pattern of behavior associated with each type of leadership. A Transformational leader seems more likely to take actions that will empower followers and make them Partners in a quest to achieve important objectives. A charismatic leader seems more likely to Emphasize the need for radical change that can only be accomplished if followers put their trust in the leader's unique expertise. Incompatible aspects of the core behaviors for transformational and charismatic leadership may make it rare for both types of leadership to occur at the same time. The Conceptual weaknesses discussed in this article suggest some revisions that are needed to improve the Theories of charismatic and transformational leadership. The focus on dyadic processes limits the utility of the theories for explaining leadership effectiveness at the group or organizational level. (House R.J.& Spangler W.D. & Woycke J. (1991). The dyadic perspective should be replaced by a systems perspective that describes leadership in terms of several distinct but inter-related influence processes at the dyadic, group, and organizational level. The inherent assumption of heroic leadership biases the theories toward explaining effectiveness in terms of the skills and actions of the leader. Transformational and charismatic leadership are often treated as equivalent, but there are plausible differences that should not be ignored or discounted. At the present time, it seems best to conceptualize the two types of leadership as distinct but partially overlapping processes. A related question is whether individual leaders can be classified into mutually exclusive categories on the basis of their use of transformational or charismatic leadership. It is still too early to determine whether there is any justification for applying labels such as "transformational" "transactional" and "charismatic" to individual leaders. (Bensman J.& Givant M. (1975).

CHAPTER 8
TEAM LEADERSHIP

The effective Team performance derives from several fundamental characteristics (Zaccaro & Klimoski, in press). First, team members need to successfully integrate their individual actions. They have specific and unique roles, where the performance of each role contributes to collective success. This means that the causes of Team failure may reside not only in member inability, but also in their collective failure, and often mediate the influences of most other exogenous variables. Secondly, Teams are increasingly required to perform in complex and dynamic environments. This Characteristic applies particularly to organizational teams, and especially to top management Teams. The operating environment for today's organizational teams features multiple stakeholders with Sometimes clashing agendas, high information load, dynamic situational contingencies, and increased Tempo of change. Advances in communication technology have made the use of virtual teams (i.e., teams whose members are not physically collocated) more practical and prominent in industry. (Adair, J. (1988). These performance requirements heighten the need for member coordination. Further, because of the greater rate of change in today's environment, team members need to operate more adaptively when coordinating their actions. Team leadership represents a third characteristic of effective Team performance. Most teams contain certain individuals who are primarily responsible for defining team goals and for developing and structuring the team to accomplish these missions. These roles exist even in self-managing teams (Nygren & Levine, 1996), although the conduct of leadership roles in such teams varies considerably from similar roles in more traditional teams. However, the success of the leader in defining team directions and organizing the team to maximize progress along such directions contributes significantly to team effectiveness. Indeed, we would argue that effective leadership processes represent perhaps the most critical factor in the success of organizational teams. Despite the ubiquity of leadership influence on organizational team performance, and despite large Literatures on both leadership (Bass, 1990, Yulk, 2002 and team group dynamics Forsyth, 1990, McGrath, 1984, we know surprisingly little about how leaders create and manage effective teams.

Previous leadership theories have tented to focus on how leaders influence collections of subordinates, Without attending to how leadership fosters the integration of subordinate actions (i.e., how leaders Promoted team processes). Path- goal theory, for example, represents an excellent example of Leadership influences on subordinate outcomes. However, it specifies the leader's role in creating Performance expectancies and valences for individual subordinates (House & Mitchell, 1974), not in Developing and maintaining effective team interaction and integration. (Alimo-Metcalfe, B.; Alban-Metcalfe, J. (2005). Most leadership theories that mention team processes treat them as moderators That indicate what leadership behaviors are most appropriate or effective in particular circumstances (e.g., Fiedler, 1964, Kerr & Jermier, 1978, Kerr et al., 1974). Accordingly, Hackman and Walton (1986) Noted," we have not found among existing leadership theories one that deals to our satisfaction with the leadership of task-performing groups in organizations. In this analysis, we present a conceptual Framework for thinking about leadership effects on team performance. We argue that leadership Processes influence team effectiveness by their effects on four sets of team processes: cognitive, Motivational, affective, and coordination. We would argue further that a number of environmental, Organizational, and team characteristics moderate the magnitude of these effects. In the next section, we present a functional model of leadership processes. We then examine how leaders influence the four aforementioned team processes. Our examination of leader-team dynamics in this disquisition rests on some central assumptions. First, we clearly presuppose hierarchical teams, having a defined leadership role, with a specified role incumbent. Most organizational teams have such structures. As noted, even most self-managing teams have supervisors who are held accountable by "higher ups" for team outcomes, and who are likely responsible for selecting team personnel, providing the team with resources and establishing the normative basis for team functioning. (Bass, B.M. (1985). The difference among team forms probably alters the specific display of particular leadership activities, but we believe that generic leadership functions apply across different kinds of teams.

FUNCTIONAL LEADERSHIP

One perspective of leadership, the functional leadership approach, specifically addresses in broad Terms the leader's relationship to the team. If a leader manages, by whatever means, to ensure that All functions critical to both task accomplishment and group maintenance are adequately taken care of, Then the leader has done his or her job well. (Alimo-Metcalfe, B.; Alban-Metcalfe. J. (2005). This Perspective defines leadership as social problem solving, where leaders are responsible for:

1. Diagnosing any problems that could potentially impede group and organizational goal attainment,
2. Generating and planning appropriate solutions, and
3. implementing solutions within typically complex social domains Fleishman et al., 1991, Mumford et al., 1993, Zaccaro et al., 1995, Zaccaro et al., in preparation.

The second distinction is that leadership typically involves discretion and choice in what solutions would be appropriated in particular problem domains. Team actions that are completely specified or fully elicited by the situation do not require the intervention of team leaders. Leadership is necessitated by team problems in which multiple solution paths are viable and/or requisite solutions need to be implemented in complex social domains through careful planning. Individuals in leadership roles are then responsible for making the choices that define subsequent team responses. We need to add a note of caution here. The definition of functional leadership suggests a tautological relationship, if the group is successful, then the leader can be defined as effective. Or any action by the leader is effective if the group succeeds. We can suggest several points that may counter this concern. First, the leadership processes that should contribute to effective group performance are a whole and its individual members. Zaccaro and Klimoski (2001) describe seven contextual imperatives that drive the nature of organizational leadership: cognitive, social, personal, political, technological, financial, and staffing. At the team level, these imperatives call for specific leader activities that are likely to be instrumental for group success and alternatively define particular leadership responses that will not contribute to group performance. Thus, group effectiveness can be theoretically defined in particular context and circumstances as a function of specific leadership actions. In other words, not just any leadership action of the contextual influences that enhance the efficacy of some leadership actions and diminishes others. Some of the propositions offered later in this account represent a step toward this task. Alternatively, we do not mean to argue that group effectiveness can be explained entirely by leadership action.

Member capabilities and skills are likely to explain a large amount of variance in team effectiveness, beyond the influence of team leadership. Likewise, leader effectiveness does not always translate into team effectiveness. Team composition and environmental or resource constraints may severely mitigate leader influence and result in team failure despite leadership efforts. Thus, the central premise of functional leadership theory is that team circumstances prescribe certain necessary leadership activities for success, while negating the utility Bennis, W. (1994). Other activities. Indeed, effective Team leaders often possess skills in defining what the critical leadership activities and responses are Or particular team situations. Information search and structuring refers to the leader's systematic search, acquisition, evaluation, and organization of information regarding team goals and operations. Information sources exist both within and outside of the team. In most organizations, for example, direct line supervisors are typically required to translate the vision and strategic intent of company executives into collective action. Information use in problem solving refers to the leader's application of acquired information to problem solving in the service of team goal attainment. After a team mission or goal is established, the leader identifies task needs and requirements, develops and evaluates possible solutions, and plans the implementation of selected solutions. Here, the team leader is responsible for translating an assigned mission into a workable plan that utilizes available team resources and accomplishes several objectives for the team. First, and perhaps foremost, an effective plan implements the solution that is the best- fitting one to the problem domain and the team's goal state.

Second, an effective plan provides a strong direction to the team such that team members have a clear Representation of performance objectives and outcomes. Third, the plan provides an "enabling performance situation" (Hackman & Walton, 1986), where adequate levels of team members' efforts, knowledge, and skills are elicited and coordinated. Further, the plan employs 'task performance strategies that are appropriate to the work, and to the setting which it is performed". A major function of team leadership is to communicate solution plans to Team members so that they understand the actions required for solution implementation, how these actions need to be coordinated, and what situation constitutes task or mission accomplishment. (Conger, L.A. (1989). The remaining two leader performance dimensions, managing personnel resources and managing material resources, include leadership activities involved in the actual implementation of developed plans and solutions. These activities are perhaps the most prominent responsibilities of organizational team leaders, particularly at lower company ranks. Managing personnel resources involves obtaining, motivating, coordinating, and monitoring the individuals under one's command. Note, however, that leader responsibilities extend beyond the motivation and orchestration of collective action. Leaders are alsoresponsible for training and developing the personnel resources under their command. Solution implementation also requires that team leaders procure adequate material resources for team action. This activity is often neglected in most classifications of leader performance functions. However, the lack of such resources will cripple team efforts, regardless of the motivation of team members and the quality of a leader's solutions and performance strategies. (Encyclopedia of Management (2009). These leader performance functions emphasize primarily the leader's recognition and construction of team problems, generation of appropriate solutions, planning the implementation of the best-fitting one, and coordinating and monitoring solution implementation. These functions represent how effective leaders respond when facilitating team goal attainment, particularly in complex and dynamic environments. A number of researchers have specified determinants of team effectiveness. Based on these models, we suggest that effective teams integrate four fundamental processes: cognitive, motivational, affective, and coordination. We propose that leadership influences on team effectiveness occur in part through them on these four processes:

1. Leadership Processes
2. Team cognitive processes
3. Information search
4. Team Motivational Processes
5. Team Effectiveness and Structuring
6. Team Affective Processes
7. Information Use
8. In Problem Solving
9. Managing Personal Resources

10. Team Coordination Processes

11. Managing Material Resources

12. Leadership and Team Processes

The model in Fig. 1 Specifies that the leader performance functions described earlier alter team Processes that contribute to team effectiveness. For example, leader information search and meaning Making can result in defining the frame of reference that team members use to understand and Complete their collective tasks. The performance strategies used by team members are most likely To emerge from leader planning and coordination activities. Likewise, their motivation and choices Regarding team effort should be influenced in part by leader exhortation and encouragement. In the Next sections, we describe key team processes in more detail and specify how leadership functions May act to facilitate these processes. (Fisk, P. (2002). The final model, and the one that is perhaps The most significant in terms of regulating team action, encodes information with respect to the individual and collective requirements for successful interactions among team members. When shared among Team members, this model, called the Team interaction model, is particularly crucial to effective coordinated action. Equipment, task, and Team mental models are presumably crucial building blocks for the Team interaction model. That is, the prescribed roles of team members need to emerge from a consideration of:

1. The equipment or other materials that team members will use in completing collective task,

2. The specific task requirements that must be addressed through collective actions, and

3. The task-relevant characteristics of team members help define the contributions each can make to roles/behavior patterns required of individual members to successfully enact collective action.

With well-developed team mental models, team members may be better able to anticipate each other's actions and reduce the amount of processing and communication required during team performance. (Goleman, D., Boyatzis, R., and Mckee, A. (2002). To achieve a high level of expertise that promotes adaptation in a dynamic operating environment, team members need to set aside time to consider, individually and collectively, the consequences of their strategies, how they considered and arrived at a team solution, and how they worked together to implement selected solutions. This is a difficult process to initiate and to complete successfully. When teams have succeeded at a task, members may not see the need for reflecting upon collective information processing and interaction patterns; likewise, when they fail, they are more likely to engage in such reflection, but it may be focused on "fixing blame," with negative consequences for subsequent team cohesion and efficacy.

LEADERSHIP AND TEAM MENTAL MODELS

A major responsibility of the Team leader is to facilitate for Team members an accurate shared Understanding of their operating environment and how, as a team, they need to respond. There has Been little, if any, research linking Team leadership to the development of effective Team mental Models. However, shared mental models of expected team and member actions serve as key mechanisms by which leaders' structure and regulate team performance. (Hersey, P. and Blanchard, P. (1969). Leaders inculcate in team members an understanding of the team's mission, the action steps Necessary to complete the mission and the role requirements for each member in collective Performance. In essence, team leaders convey their own understandings and mental models of the problem situation as derived from their boundary spanning activities. Thus, leadership processes and the quality of a team Leader's mental models become determinants of subsequent team mental models. Further, team mental models mediate the influence of leadership on team coordination and team performance. The critical point of this leader- team influence is the leader's sense-making activities on behalf of the Team. Sense making can be defined as being "about such things as the placement of items into frameworks, comprehending, redressing surprise, constructing meaning, interacting in the pursuit of mutual understanding, and patterning." (House, R. J. (1971). Sense-making and sense-giving processes include extracting important environmental cues, placing these cues in a team' performance context, and embellishing the meaning of these cues into a coherent framework. This framework provides team members an enriched mental model of cue response contingencies, linked to environmental events, and includes the meaning or rationale for why certain collective actions are more or less appropriate in different situations. It is this last feature of sense making that produces shared mental models. Promoting team adaptation in a dynamic environment. The arguments suggest a process of leader-team performance that begins with the development of a leader's mental representation of a problem situation. This mental model reflects not only the components of the problem confronting the team, but also the environmental and organizational contingencies that define the larger context of team action. Here, the leader develops a model of what the team problem is and what solutions are possible in this context, given particular environmental and organizational constraints and resources.

LEADERSHIP AND COLLECTIVE INFORMATION PROCESSING

Team leaders are also responsible for facilitating the information processing activities engaged by the team as it accomplishes its task. The most potent leadership processes that foster collective information processes include encouraging and coaching team members to engage in problem identification, diagnosis, solution generation, and solution selection activities(Kozlowski et al., 1996). As teams mature and move from a training/learning focus to a more action or performance orientation, leader roles shift to fostering team self-management, particularly in terms of problem-solving activities. (Kozlowski,(1998). Argues that as teams enter performance environments, "leaders are not so much responsible for directing specific team actions as they are responsible for developing the underlying individual and team capabilities that enable teams to self-manage their actions.

Team Motivational Processes

Team effectiveness is grounded in members being motivated to work hard on behalf of the team. This Motivation derives in part from the cohesion of the team and from its sense of collective efficacy.

PERFORMANCE NORMS

Both task-based cohesion and collective efficacy are associated with strong work norms. Some groups establish a climate that compels hard work from their members. Norms develop in such groups that call for strong effort and higher performance from all group members. Once established, these norms are enforced by the members themselves; when deviations occur, members will communicate in various ways with the nonconforming individual to bring him or her in line with group work expectations. (Sills, D. L. (Ed) 1991).

LEADERSHIP AND TEAM MOTIVATION

Leadership and team motivation indicates the influences of specific leader functions on team Motivational processes. In essence, leaders raise team motivation both directly by a number of motivational strategies, and indirectly through their planning, coordinating personnel development, and feedback behaviors.

- Leadership Processes
- Team Task Cohesion
- Planning and Goal Setting
- Team Effectiveness
- Coordinating Performance
- Strategies
- Developing Team Members
- Motivating Team Members

- Collective Efficacy
- Providing Feedback

Finally, Team efficacy emerges from the leader's effective accomplishment of the leadership functions listed in Table 1. These functions enhance the likelihood that leaders and their teams will build a history of successful accomplishment and increase their sense of competence. They examined the leader's efficacy to complete leadership functions, the goals and strategies they establish for the group, their display of leadership functions, and their group's cohesion, collective efficacy, and performance on a Simulated manufacturing game. They found that the leader's sense of efficacy and the goals and strategies they established influenced how they interacted with the team. Their goals and subsequent team-directed actions, in turn, influenced the team's collective efficacy. These leadership processes also had direct effects on the team's cohesion (after controlling for prior performance) and subsequent performance. Finally, to demonstrate the adaptiveness of these processes, Kane et al. varied the complexity of the team's operating environment. They found that leadership influences on the team were stronger under higher team complexity. Other studies have demonstrated significant linkages among leadership behavior, team efficacy and team performance. He suggested that this early influence was a function of the leader's own efficacy regarding the team, and of the leader's meaning-making behaviors that contribute to the reduction of ambiguity early in the team's subsequent performance. These effects of team emotions can be beneficial for team effectiveness if they result in processes that foster more effective group interactions. Teams performing under stressful conditions can be highly susceptible to emotional distress across team members. As team environments become more aversive (i.e., more time-urgent, stressful, complex, ambiguous), Team members obviously need to maintain a collective calm. Teams are not likely to be able to avoid environmental stressors; to be effective, they need to develop collective coping mechanisms that foster continued effectiveness, even under stress.

CHAPTER 9

HOW LEADERS CREATE AND USE NETWORKS?

The first helped them manage current internal responsibilities, the second boosted their personal Development, and the third opened their eyes to new business directions and the stakeholders they Would need to enlist. While our managers differed in how well they pursued operational and personal Networking, we discovered that almost all of them underutilized strategic networking. In this Commodity, we describe key features of each networking form (summarized in the exhibit "the three Forms of networking") and, using our manager's experiences, explain how a three-pronged networking strategy can become part and parcel of a new leader's development plan. (Aral, S., & Van Alstyne, M. (2011).

THE THREE FORMS OF NETWORKING

Managers who think they are adept at networking are often operating only at an operational or Personal Level. Effective leaders learn to employ networks for strategic purposes.

1. Operational
2. Personal
3. Strategic

Purpose Enhancing personal Figuring out priorities & challenges; & professional development getting stakeholder support for them. Getting work done; providing referrals to useful information & contacts. Efficiently, Contacts are mostly external and oriented toward current interests and future potential interests. Maintaining the capacities and functions required of the group.

Location and temporal orientation: contacts are mostly internal and oriented toward current demands etc. All managers need to build good working relationships with the people who can help them do their jobs. The number and breadth of people involved can be impressive such operational networks include not Only direct reports and superiors but also peers within an operational unit, other internal players with the power to block or support a project, and key outsiders such as suppliers, distributors, and customers. The purpose of this type of networking is to ensure coordination and cooperation among people who have to know and trust one another in order to accomplish their immediate tasks. That isn't always easy, but it is relatively straightforward, because the task provides focus and a clear criterion for membership in the network: Either you are necessary to the job and helping to get it done, or you are not. Although operational networking was the form that came most naturally to the managers we studied, nearly everyone had important blind spots regarding people and groups they depended on to make things happen. In one case, Alicia, an accounting manager who worked in an entrepreneurial firm with several hundred employees, was suddenly promoted by the company's founder to financial director and given a seat on the board. He was both the youngest and the least-experienced board member, and his instinctive response to these new responsibilities was to reestablish his functional credentials. (Aron, A., Melinat, E, N., Vaollone, R., & Bator, R. (1997). Acting on a hint from the founder that the company might go public, Alicia undertook a reorganization of the accounting department that would enable the books to withstand close scrutiny. Alicia succeeded brilliantly in upgrading his team's capabilities, but he missed the fact that only a minority of the seven-person board shared the founder's ambition.

A year into Alicia's tenure, discussion about whether to take the company public polarized the board, and he discovered that all that time cleaning up the books might have been better spent sounding out his co-directors. One of the problems with an exclusive reliance on operational networks is that they are usually geared toward meeting objectives as assigned, not toward asking the strategic question," what should we be doing?" By the same token, managers do not exercise as much personal choice in assembling operational relationship as they do in weaving personal and strategic networks, because to a large extent the right relationships are prescribed by the job and organizational structure. Thus, most operational networking occurs within an organization, and ties are determined in large part by routine, short-term demands. Relationships formed with outsiders, such as board members, customers, and regulators, are directly task-related and tend to be bounded and constrained by demands determined at a higher level. Of course, an individual manager can choose to deepen and develop the ties to different extents, and all managers exercise discretion over who gets priority attention. It's the quality of relationships, the rapport and mutual trust that gives an operational network its power. Nonetheless, the substantial constraints on network membership mean these connections are unlikely to deliver value to managers beyond assistance with the task at hand. As a manager moves into a leadership role, his /her network must reorient itself externally and toward the future. (Burt, R. S. (1992).

The typical manager in our group was more concerned with sustaining cooperation with the existing Network than with building relationships to face nonroutine or unforeseen challenges. But as a Manager moves into a leadership role, his/her network must reorient itself externally and toward the future as well.

PERSONAL NETWORKING

We observed that once aspiring leaders like Alicia awaken to the dangers of an excessively internal Focus, they begin to seek kindred spirits outside their organizations. Simultaneously, they become aware of the limitations of the limitations of their social skills, such as a lack of knowledge about professional domains beyond their own, which makes it difficult for them to find common ground with people outside their usual circles. Through professional associations, alumni groups, clubs, and personal interest communities, managers gain new perspectives that allow them to advance in their careers. This is what we mean by personal networking. Many of the managers we study question why they should spend precious time on an activity so indirectly related to the work at hand. Why widen one's circle of casual acquaintances when there isn't time even for urgent tasks? The answer is that these contacts provide important referrals, information, and, often, developmental support such as coaching and mentoring. A newly appointed factory director, for Example, faced with a turnaround or close -down situation that was paralyzing his staff, joined a business organization and through it met a lawyer who became his counsel in the turnaround. Buoyed by his success, he networked within his company's headquarters in search of someone who had dealt with a similar crisis. Eventually, he found two mentors. A personal network can also be a safe space for personal development and as such can provide a foundation for strategic networking. The experience of Willy, a principal in a midsize software company, is a good example. Like his father, Willy stuttered. When he had the opportunity to prepare for meetings, his stutter was not an issue, but spontaneous Encounters inside and outside the company were dreadfully painful. To solve this problem, he began accepting at least two invitations per week to the social gatherings he had assiduously ignored before. Before each event, he asked who else had been invited and did background research on the other Guests so that he could initiate conversations. The hardest part, he said was" getting through the door."

Once inside, his interest in the conversations helped him forget himself and master his stutter. As his stutter diminished, he also applied himself to networking across his company, whereas previously he had taken refuse in his technical expertise. Like Willy, several of our emerging leaders successfully used personal networking as a relatively safe way to expose problems and seek insight into solutions safe, that is, compared with strategic networking, in which the stakes are far higher. Personal networks are largely external, made up of discretionary links to people with whom we have something in common. As a result, what makes a personal network powerful is its referral potential. According to the famous Six degrees of separation principle, our personal contacts are valuable to the extent that they help us reach, in as few connections as possible, the far-off person who has the information we need. In watching managers struggle to widen their professional relationship in ways that feel both natural and legitimate to them, we repeatedly saw them shift their time and energy from operational to personal networking. For people who have rarely looked outside their organizations, this is an important first step, one that fosters a deeper understanding of themselves and the environments in which they move.

Ultimately, however, personal networking alone won't propel managers through the leadership transition. Aspiring leaders may find people who awaken new interests but fail to become comfortable with the power players at the level. Above them. Or they may achieve new influence within a professional community but fail to harness those ties in the service of organizational goals. That's why managers who know they need to develop their networking skills, and make a real effort to do so, nonetheless may end up feeling like they have wasted their time and energy. As we'll see, personal networking will not help a manager through the leadership transition unless he or she learns how to bring those connections to bear on organizational strategy. (Burt, R. S. (2012).

STRATEGIC NETWORKING

When managers begin the delicate transition from functional manager to business leader, they must start to concern themselves with broad strategic issues. Lateral and vertical relationships with other functional and business unit managers, all people outside their immediate control, become a lifeline for figuring out how their own contributions fit into the big picture. Thus, strategic networking plugs the aspiring leader into a set of relationships and information sources that collectively embody the power to achieve personal and organizational goals.

INDISTINCTION TO FUNCTIONAL MANAGER TO BUSINESS LEADER: HOW COMPANIES CAN HELP?

Executives who oversee management development know how to spot critical inflection points:

The moments when highly successful people must change their perspective on what is important and, Accordingly, how they spend their time. Many organizations still promote people on the basis of their Performance in roles whose requirements differ dramatically from those of leadership roles. And many New leaders feel that they are doing it alone, without coaching or guidance. By being sensitive to the Fact that most strong technical or functional managers lack the capabilities required to build strategic Networks that advance their personal and professional goals, human resources and learning Professional can take steps to help in this important area. Operating beside players with diverse Affiliations, backgrounds, objectives, and incentives requires a manager to formulate business rather Than functional objectives, and to work through the coalitions and networks needed to sell ideas and compete for resources. Consider Monica, a manager who, after rising steadily through the ranks in Logistics and distribution, was stupefied to learn that the CEO was considering a radical reorganization of her function that would strip her of some responsibilities. Rewarded to date for incremental annual improvements, she had failed to notice shifting priorities in the wider market and the resulting internal shuffle for resources and power at the higher levels of her company. Although she had built a loyal, high- performing Team, she had few relationships outside her group to help her anticipate the new imperatives, let alone give her ideas about how to respond. After she argued that distribution issues were her purview, and failed to be persuasive, she hired consultants to help her prepare a counterproposal. But Monica's boss simply concluded that she lacked a broad, longer-term business strategic projects, Team building, change management projects, and in-depth discussions with business leaders from inside and outside the company. (Campbell, M., & Smith, R. (2010). The young leaders who participate end up with a strong internal and external nexus of ties to support them as their careers evolve. Companies that recognize the importance of leadership networking can also do a lot to help people overcome their innate discomfort by creating natural ways for them to extend their networks. When Toyota CEO Akio Toyoda of Toyota Motor Sought to break down crippling internal barriers at the company, he created cross-functional Teams of middle managers from diverse units and charged them with proposing solutions to problems ranging from supply costs to product design. Toyota subsequently institutionalized the Teams, not just as a way to solve problems but also to encourage lateral networks. Rather than avoid the extra work, aspiring leaders ask for these assignments. Most professional development is based on the notion that successful people acquire new role appropriate. Skills as they move up the hierarchy. But making the transition from manager to leader requires subtraction as well as addition: To make room for new competencies, managers must rely less on their perspective on how to perspective. Frustrated, Monica contemplated leaving the company. Only after some patient coaching from a senior manager did she understand that she had to get out of her unit and start talking to opinion leaders inside and outside the company to form a sellable plan for the future. (Cross, R. L., & Parker, A. (2004). What differentiates a leader from a manager, research tells us, is the ability to figure there. Recruiting stakeholders, lining up allies and sympathizers, diagnosing the political landscape, and brokering conversations among unconnected parties are all part of a leader's job. As they step up to the leadership transition, some managers accept their growing dependence on others and seek to transform it into mutual influence. Others dismiss such work as "political" and, as a result, undermines their ability to advance their goals. Several of the participants in our sample chose the latter approach, justifying their choice as a matter of personal values and integrity. In one case, Judith, who managed a department in a large company under what she described as "dysfunctional" leadership, refused even to try to activate her extensive network within the firm when internal adversaries took over key functions of her unit. When we asked her why she didn't seek help from anyone in the organization to stop this coup, she replied that she refused to play "stupid political games, you can only do what you think is the ethical and right thing from your perspective. "stupid or not, those games cost her the respect and support of her direct reports and coworkers, who hesitated to follow someone they perceived as unwilling to defend herself. Eventually she had no choice but to leave. The key to a good strategic network is leverage: the ability to marshal information, support, and resources from one sector of a network to achieve results in another. Strategic networkers use indirect influence, convincing one person in the network to get someone else, who is not in the network, to take a needed action. More over, strategic networkers don't just influence their relational environment; they shape it in their own image by moving and hiring subordinates, changing suppliers and sources of financing, lobbying to place allies in peer positions, and even restructuring their boards to create networks favorable to their business goals. Judith abjured such tactics, but her adversaries did not. Strategic networking can be difficult for emerging leaders because it absorbs a significant amount of the time and energy that managers usually devote to meeting their many operational demands. This is one reason why many managers drop their strategic networking precisely when they need it most: when their units are in trouble and only outside support can rescue them. The trick is not to hide in the operational network but to develop it into a more strategic one. One manager we studied, for example, used lateral and functional contracts throughout his firm to resolve tensions with his boss that resulted from substantial differences in style and strategic approaches between the two. (Cross, R., Thomas, R. J., & Light, D. A. (2008). Tied down in operational chores at a distant location, the manager had lost Contact with headquarters. He resolved the situation by simultaneously obliging his direct reports to Take on more of the local management effort and sending messages through his network that would Bring him back into the loop with the boss. Operational, personal, and strategic networks are not Mutually exclusive. One manager we studied used his personal passion, hunting, to meet people from Professions as diverse as stonemasonry and household moving. Almost none of these hunting friends Had anything to do with his work in the consumer electronics industry, yet they all had to deal with One of his own daily concerns: customer relations. Hearing about their problems and techniques allowed him to view his own from a different perspective and helped him define principles that he could test in his work. Ultimately, what began as a personal network of hunting partners became operationally and strategically valuable to this manager. The key was his ability to build inside and outside links for maximum leverage. But we've seen others who avoided networking, or failed at it, because they let interpersonal chemistry, not strategic needs, determine which relationships they cultivated.

CHAPTER 10
GROUP LEVEL THEORIES

WHAT ARE THE THREE GROUP THEORIES?

T he theory is based on the belief that when people get together in a group, there are three main Interpersonal needs they are looking to obtain, inclusion in the group, affection and openness, and Control.

Group Theory

There is the saying that "we come into the world alone and leave alone and everything else is a gift." Whilst our significant one to one relationship are crucial to our emotional wellbeing, it is an Understanding of who we are with groups, family work or social, that is at least as important to good Emotional health. The purpose of this object is to go through a few of the key theories around groups, how groups develop, group conflict, some personal thoughts and experiences, and signpost to additional resources. (Calhoun, Craig J., (ed.) (2010). When people join together in any kind of group setting, it becomes a living and growing entity. Some people act quite differently in a group setting to the way they act with people and can either thrive or struggle with the different dynamics and form that group relationships take to 1-1. When people work together in a group, all sorts of things happen: allegiances are made, cliques formed within the wider group, there are issues around control and dominance, and sometimes "scapegoating" of an individual (s) can take place; this is what is referred to as the group process or group dynamic, and often gets overlooked in work settings for the apparent" chalice" of the task.

There are a number of aspects of the group process or group dynamic including: Patterns of communication and coordination within the group. Patterns of influence. Roles/relationship of people within the group. Patterns of dominance (e.g. who leads, who defers). The balance of task focuses versus social focus. The level of group effectiveness, and the clarity of what the group is there to do. How conflict is handled within the group. The emotional state of the group as a whole, or what Wilfred Bion called "basic assumptions."

Foundation Group Theory
Systems Theory

Systems theory finds commonalities between individual beings and groups of beings. The theory sees Groups as living systems that connect, work together, and evolve over time. Relationships are Constantly interacting and changing both within and between themselves. Whilst group boundaries Provide some stability, they are open to various life forces which pull and pull on the group; a" stormy Sea of changes both within and outside the group" Some core principles of system theory applied to groups are:. Interpersonal systems are holistic: as people we need social bonds and relationships for our emotional Wellbeing. Most people have strong bonds with formal and informal groups such as couples, families, Circles of friends, work groups, community groups etc. (Mustafa Sheriff (1953). When people come Together in a group a psychological boundary develops around them and separates them from other People, and can often make them stronger and different; consider the less skillful teams that win Championships as they work together as a strong unit, or the evidence that family experts now Recognize that the health of the whole family must be improved in order to help individual members. The principles also work on the basis of "complementary"; that each member of the group makes a Beneficial contribution of ideas which are not available otherwise; each member is needed, and no one Is there by accident. Group systems are always changing as changes happen for individuals, this impacts on them, and creates a v: vibration "which results in change in a group. This can lead from a period of stability to stress, to a period of dissonance, and then finally to change. This change cycle helps groups constantly change to things happening within and outside the group. Systems theory also sees groups through lifespan changes including birth and infancy, early Development, adolescence, maturity, ageing and disintegration, when the group is no longer viable. Pattern dependency; groups over time tend to develop a self-organizing nature which works to maintain stability and minimize threats. They create patterns to meet needs, cope with stress and conflict, and to deal with the demands from outside. The early spontaneity of relationships is replaced by a reliance on patterns, and an unwillingness to change. (T D Kemper (1968).

GROUP DEVELOPMENT AND PHASES

The goal of most research on group development is to learn why and how small groups change over time. To do this, researchers examine patterns of change and continuity in groups over time. Aspects of a group that might be studied include the quality of the output produced by a group, the type and frequency of its activities, its cohesiveness, the existence of conflict, amongst others. Perhaps the best known of these models is Tuckers 4 stage model for teams, designed in 1965:

Forming

As the team forms, members tend to be on their "best behavior" and work on getting along storming as the team gets closer, conflict develops. Disagreements build and cliques appear. Norming Rules of conduct develop, and members discuss their differences rather than argue. Performing As the team reaches maturity, members are open and supportive of each other.

Group Dynamic Process – Tuckmann Disintegrating Out Performaing

- Norming
- Storming
- Forming
- Time

Define Team Coaching

Over the last couple of years, I have become increasingly involved in coaching Teams in addition to 1-1 Coaching work with people and become more interested in the range of approaches to work effectiveness with Teams. I have also reflected that whilst certain principles seem to work, there are a number of different ways to go about the work; what works with one team often doesn't work with another. Essentially, Team Coaching works with the team as a system as opposed to a collection of individuals and is an ongoing process to sustain change over time as opposed to a one-off Team building event. I have increasing concerns about the idea of a "fix it all in one day" approach to Team building, as time and time again the question of sustaining actions and behaviors agreed by the Team at initial day requires an ongoing level of reflection and time out from the team. Team coaching helps people understand how to work better with others. It's an effective method for Showing Teams how to reduce conflict and improve their working relationships. There are some Team Coaching interventions that primarily focus on the interactions and working relationships: the way People act with their Teammates, and the way they communicate with one another, these are important drivers of effective Team performance. However, there are others that stress the need to start by clarifying the primary purpose of the Team, its goals and objectives, and the role of the people in the Team before looking at team dynamics and relationships.

AGREEING THE METRICS AND ASSESSMENT FOR THE PROGRAMME

My approach would be to ensure a strong level of alignment with organizational vision and strategy, and how the team is planning to work towards that. This makes the intervention easier to measure. Approaches I have used with Team coaching has been to re-visit the purpose and vision of the Team, and if necessary, support the team to create a Team plan with objectives in the areas of strategy, finance, marketing, working with external stakeholders etc. It obviously depends on what the stated need of the Team is, but getting the Team to focus on some basic functions of the Team is often important. (Cooley, (1902). It is vital to include the "softer skills" development areas of the Team such as improved Teamwork and morale, enhanced communication skills or increased engagement from staff within the wider Team (especially if the Team being coached is a Leadership Team). As far as the metrics for the Team coaching are concerned these may include areas such as:

- Development of Key Leadership Skills across the Team
- Improvement in Relationships & Increased Trust
- A Sense of Shared/Common Issues
- Assessing how the Coaching has Provided a Vehicle for Culture Change
- The Amount of Time spent on "Real/Pressing" Issues
- Creation of approaches to sustainability, such as long-term peer coaching.

It is usually helpful to have a combination of team-based task objectives and working relationships/Team dynamics.

TEAM COACHING

Diagnostic "Kick off" Foundation Discovery interviews Create a contract with the team, With the team, along with any including agreed measures of success. Establish the diagnostic assessments to be used (e.g. 360, Foundation for psychometrics) Coaching sessions

The initiative; Frequency of sessions, approach to the sessions, Strategic objectives, usually over 6- 9 month period Nature of team Assessment and sustainability Dynamics, Repeat diagnostic assessment Timeline Reflect on sustaining the Team to internalize coaching practice Most of the models I have researched and my own practice has covered some or all of the main steps Listed below, and the diagram above is my suggested approach. These steps are indicative, and not all steps are mandatory or sequential, depending on the needs of the Team. Establish the foundation for the initiative; strategic objectives, nature of team dynamics, timeline.

Diagnostic Approaches

- Often initial 1-1 confidential meetings with Team members to find out what works well for the team, what doesn't and why to establish their ideas on approaches that will work, and how they could be measured.

- Going into a Team development initiative of any kind without these having the opportunity to engage With the Team is very hard. In terms of "diagnostic assessment" approaches, personality and behavior assessments like insights are good tools for improving a Team's understanding of its own dynamics, and they give team members a better understanding of why they react to their colleagues in certain ways. This new understanding helps them think about how they can relate to one another more effectively, at the same time that it breeds tolerance by helping people understand that different approaches may be valid in different situations.

"KICK OFF"

- Focus on the wider organizational aspect, as well as the Team challenge.

- Create Team contract, including the metrics and assessment for the program (individual and Team)

- Determine areas of focus and commitment for the sessions.

ONGOING COACHING SESSIONS

- Group size 6 to 8 is the ideal size for a Team, with a maximum of around 11.12
- Frequency, around once monthly
- Duration, often around 6 months, though can be shorter or longer.
- Decision on how to run the sessions in terms of level of formality. Action Learning set approach focuses.

On improving questioning and reflection of Team members and is proven to be a quick trust builder, but some sessions may be more formal than others, where a coaching tool is used, like insights or Belbin, or a Team Coaching Wheel. ("Merton & Kitt 1950, pp. 50-51).

WHAT HAPPENS BETWEEN SESSIONS?

- A sustainable way of encouraging ongoing coaching support is through peer coaching which helps keep Focus between sessions, and accountability developed with peers.
- Members of the Team are encouraged to exchange with direct reports and gain feedback.

ASSESSMENT AND SUSTAINABILITY

- It's important to review the "distance traveled" of the Team coaching project for the whole Team and the individuals in it, and the strongest way to do this is to repeat the baseline assessment, whether its 360 or psychometric.
- Its important to look at ways beyond the Team coaching project that the reflective practice of the Team is sustained;

e.g. regular reviews using Learning set principles, ongoing peer coaching. Each Team member is requested to both give feedback and to receive feedback. The feedback is facilitated by the coach. It's also wise for the coach to take notes during the process. Each Team member takes in turn on the "hot seat". They cannot say anything, ask anything (unless they haven't heard the comment) on any of the feedback they receive. Once on the hot seat they listen to each Team member giving feedback. The feedback is around what the Team would like the person in the hot Seat to "stop, start and continue" doing. The team member gets off the "hot seat" and another Team member takes their place.

What are behavioral change models and theories?

Group theory is the study of groups. Groups are sets equipped with an operation (like multiplication, addition, or composition) that satisfies certain basic properties. Symmetry groups appear in the study of combinatorics overview and algebraic number theory b, as well as physics and chemistry.

What are behavioral change models and theories?

Behavioral change theories are attempts to explain why behavior changes. Whereas models of behavior Are more diagnostic and geared towards understanding the psychological factors that explain or predict a specific behavior, theories of change are more process-oriented and generally aimed at changing a given behavior. Social identify theory is built on three key cognitive components: social categorization, social identification, and social comparison.

CHAPTER 11
LEADER ORGANIZATION AND COORDINATION THE ACTIVITIES OF TEAM MEMBERS

What are the three most important things needed for effective Teamwork in the Workplace?

There are five elements of successful Teamwork.

- Communication: Effective communication is the most important part of teamwork and involves consistently updating each person and never assuming that everyone has the same information. Delegation; Teams that work well together understand the strengths and weaknesses of each Team Member.

- Efficiency

- Ideas

There are seven key Elements to a successful Team coordination One of the most exciting tasks for a leader is to achieve a successful coordination within her/his Team. Like in most companies, for example, in Disney world, the work is performed by a Team, and we try to make each task fit the other ones in the best way possible. In this regard, I've learnt that there is a list of elements that every leader should take into account: We have to note some important methods of leading for example: The key is communication, Events, Features, Goals, help, Leadership, Marketing, Methodologies, Monitor, Organization, planning, Productivity and project Management etc. Having a global picture of all the work that has to be done.

1. The Leader must have a long-term vision of the tasks that have to be performed. Her/his attitude should Be more "visionary" in order to be ahead of the needs of the company and the Team, in that way she/He can provide quick responses to changes and unforeseen aspects that can appear in the future.

2. Setting a common goal. There is no point in coordinating a team if we don't know what we want to achieve.

3. Knowing your Team

   The members of a Team are, in most cases, very different between them. Everyone has her/his Own way of thinking or acting. That's why, for a project leader, it is very important to know Each Team member. It allows assigning tasks according to the strengths of each member, reinforcing their motivation and supporting their specialization in a direct and positive way.

4. Defining Team Roles

   Is a task tightly linked to the previous point. Each Team member plays a particular role within the organization and we can only create a strong and consolidated Team if we achieve that Each person has the role that better fits their flairs and skills.

5. Planning

   Once the Team is formed and the role of each Team member defined, we should make a Planning that includes all the tasks to perform, the estimated time and, where is needed, the Development of events. (Agarwal, R. (2003).

6. Communicating

As you can imagine, all the previous points will lose their sense if we haven't been able to transmit them to the Team. In order to achieve this, it will be necessary to hold meetings. It's important to make meetings as productive as possible, that is why one should clearly define their contents beforehand, so stalled situations or backwards steps are avoided.

7. Finding the correct tools

It is evident that we should make use of all tools that can make the work of coordination easier. In particular there are applications which let us define what tasks are to be performed, who Is assigned to them and when they have to be finished. In addition, if we communicate the Information to the Team, we'll reduce unproductive and unnecessary meetings. Disney world is a clear example of a tool that helps you. Nobody says that it'll be easy, but you should Try to escape from complexity, and, thanks to Disney world, you can do it. There is no doubt that to perform a correct management activity some skills are necessary. This is related to the old, everlasting question about if these skills are innate or we can learn them. From my perspective, no one is perfect and everything can be improved. The really important thing is to be sure of What you want to do and do it well. Surround yourself with the best teammates, learn, make mistakes and correct them. That is the only way to better yourself and get closer to perfection. Do you agree with these elements? Would you like to add any other? We'd like to hear your ideas! (Harris& Harris (1996). Teamwork has always been an essential capability for successful Enterprises, but with today's organizations undergoing and digitization in an" innovate or die' Economy, it is now more important than ever that employees can collaborate effectively across Geographical sites, between business functions and within increasingly fluid job hierarchies. Successful Team work is also an important for employee engagement and wellbeing at a time When talent retention faces the highly competitive global job market as well as the "loyalty challenge" posed by millennial workers.

Here are the keys of the Teams in the future:

1. Communication

   Effective communication is the most important part of teamwork and involves consistently Updating each person and assuming that everyone has the same information. Being a good Communicator also means being a good listener; by listening to your colleagues, you show Them respect, which is an essential trust-building method. Offering encouragement also goes a long way to getting the best out of team members. Collaborating and being open to new ideas are also essential ingredients for a harmonious Team environment.

2. Delegation

   Teams that work well together understand the strengths and weaknesses of each Team members.

3. Efficiency

   A strong and cohesive Team develops systems that allow them to collaborate efficiency to complete tasks in a timely manner. Through working together, colleagues will be aware of their own capabilities and the capabilities of the group in general and can organize the workload accordingly.

4. Ideas

   When a Team works well together, colleagues feel more comfortable offering suggestions and ideas. A respectful and trusting Team environment will not only enable colleagues to think more creatively But will lead to more productive and collaborative brainstorming sessions.

5. Support

   All work-places provide challenges, but having a strong Team environment in place can act as a support Mechanism for staff members. They can help each other improve their own performance as well as working together toward improving their professional development. Building bonds on trust and reliance on each other can be extremely important when facing a particular difficult challenge or if the group is forced to deal with the loss of a Team member while continuing to maintain productivity. Good Team work means a synergistic way of working with each person committed and working towards a shared goal. Teamwork maximizes the individual strengths of Team members to bring out their best. It is therefore a necessity that leaders facilitate and build the Teamwork skills of their people if they Are to steer a company toward success.

WHAT ARE THE THREE (3) MOST IMPORTANT ROLES OF A LEADER?

Three Roles of Leaders

   1. Understanding Leadership
   2. Goal
   3. Envisioning

To experience and conceptualize three important leadership processes aligning others toward the vision; and ensuring execution or implementation.

Group Size: 15-30 participants
Time Required: Approximately 90 minutes
Materials:

Physical Setting:
Process:
Variation:

How do you manage a Successful Team?

The 10 Golden Rules of Effective Management

1. Be Consistent
2. Focus on clarity, accuracy and thoroughness in communication
3. Set the goal of working as a Team
4. Publicly reward and recognize hardwork
5. Be the Example
6. Never go with "One size fit all"
7. Remain as transparent as possible
8. Encourage all opinions and ideas

What are the five criteria for successful Team Performance?

The key elements to successful Teamwork are trust, Communication and effective Leadership; a focus on common goals with a collective responsibility for success (or failure).

What are the Roles of a Team Leader?

A Team Leader is someone who provides guidance, instruction, direction and leadership to A group of individuals (the Team) for the purpose of achieving a key result or group of Aligned results. When a team leader motivates a team, group members can function in a Goal oriented manner.

What are the Roles of a Good Leader?

Leadership is the action of leading employees to achieve goals. It plays an important role in employee and productivity. A good leader: Sets a clear vision by influencing employees to understand and accept the future state of the organization.

How do you motivate your Team?

Try these 9 powerful Ways to keep the members of your Team motivated and giving their very best on the job.

1. Pay your people what they are worth
2. Provide them with a pleasant place to work
3. Offer opportunities for self-development
4. Foster collaboration with the Team
5. Encourage Happiness
6. Don't punish failure
7. Set Clear Goals

How can employees improve their performance?

Here are the top 10 things you can do to increase employee efficiency at the office:

- Don't be Afraid to Delegate
- Match Tasks to Skills
- Communicate Effectively
- Keep Goals Clear & Focused
- Incentivize Employees
- Cut Out the Excess
- Train and Develop Employees
- Embrace Telecommuting

Goes on with it. While there is nothing wrong with prioritizing quality (it is what makes a Business successful, after all), checking over every small detail yourself rather than delegating Can waste everyone's valuable time. Instead, give responsibilities to qualified employees, and Trust that they will perform the tasks well. This and your employees the opportunity to gain Skills and leadership experience that will ultimately benefit your company. You hired them for A reason, now give them a chance to prove you right. Match tasks to skills- Knowing your employees' skills and behavioral styles is essential for maximizing efficiency.

TOP 10 WAYS TO IMPROVE EMPLOYEE EFFICIENCY

As daylight savings approaches, it's a good time to think about different ways you can, well, Save time. These days, employees are spending more and more time at the office certainly Exceeding the typical 40-hour work week. However, increasing the hours worked does not necessarily translate to increased efficiency. So, how can leaders and managers improve employee efficiency at the office.

1. Don't be Afraid to Delegate

While this tip might seem the most obvious, it is often the most difficult to put into Practice. We get it your company is your baby, so you want to have a direct hand in in Very thing that methods are as efficient as possible, right? Not necessarily. A Mckinsey study found that emails can take up nearly 28% of an employee's time. In fact, email was revealed to be the second most time consuming activity for workers (after their job-specific tasks). Instead of relying solely on email, try social networking tools (such as slack) designed for even quicker Team communication. (Adair, J. (1988). You can also encourage your employees to occasionally adopt a more antiquated form of contact, voice to voice communication. Having a quick meeting or phone call can settle a matter that might have taken hours of back-and-forth emails. Let them know exactly what you expect of them and tell them specifically what impact this assignment will have.

2. Incentivize Employees

One of the best ways to encourage employees to be more efficient is to actually give them a reason to do so. Recognizing your workers for a job well done will make them feel appreciated and encourage them to continue increasing their productivity. When deciding how to reward efficient employees, make sure you take into account their individual needs or preferences. For example, one employee might appreciate public recognition. While another would prefer a private "thank you". In addition to simple words of gratitude, here are a few incentives you can try. Increasing employee efficiency isn't all about what they can do better, some of the responsibility falls on you as well. But just like your employees, you aren't psychic. So, after reviewing your employees, ask them what you could do to help them improve. Maybe they would like a little more guidance on certain tasks or would prefer a little more room for creative freedom. Asking for feedback not only gives you clear, immediate ways to help your employees improve, but also encourages a culture of open dialogue that will allow for continued development over time.

Shared beliefs about desirable end states or modes of conduct in a given culture "what cultures are like "capabilities associated with visual and mental representation of objectives in space. Refers to the degree to which members believe that the team can be effective across a variety of situations and tasks. Step two of the change process, change itself is implemented. First step in the change process; Individuals must be shown why the change is necessary. Involves training members in the duties and Responsibilities of their Teammates. Gross body equilibrium performing stage in team dev. In which members experience anxiety and other emotions as they disengage and ultimately separate from the Team.

MANAGERS VS LEADERS

Manager- organized, planning Leader- Works with staff, respected. Charisma, Intelligence, drive, organized, self-confidence, integrity, flexibility. One person assumes all Authority and responsibility, directive, command and control. Leader gathers info. And opinions of members before making decisions, makes decisions after receiving input, must be willing to Share credit of success. Decision made by majority of group. Types of decisions made, policies and procedures hiring new staff, development of marketing strategies. Requires decisions or plans made by group based on all members working together until agreement is reached most associated with women managers ex Juries, search committees. Coach an individual on how to become a leader and be comfortable giving their input. Transforming a person to move up high position. Success planning" setting employee up with leadership attributes. Group of people who do not have Manager in charge, usually temporary cost efficient self- managed Teams work on a specific issue, not Day-to-day things. Determines goals, missions, deadlines and processes for a specific project. Planning Determine what should happen, develop mission / goals. Blueprint. Organizing, coordinate relationships, resources, activities, establish method dealing with issues- leading, create environment which motivates members to contribute to achieve organizational goals. Staffing- recruit, select, train, and retention controlling ensure plans are being followed, create standards inspect work to ensure standards are met. Frontline Manager- oversee production, customer contact, ex.: front desk- middle manager-oversee group of workers and supervisors, ex.: sales manager. Top-level manager-direct activities of large. Organization, Ex.: CEO or GM. – Interpersonal manager acts as figurehead, leader/liaison (managing Through people). Informational monitor, disseminate, spoke person (managing through info.). Decisional, entrepreneur, disturbance handler, resource allocation, negotiator (managing through action. Chain of command vertical relationship, ind. Report ideas to supervisor everyone knows their place. Span of control measures influence manager has on its staff determined by number of people manager is responsible for Centralization. Concentrate of decision making and power focus at upper level of organization (consistence VS Slow to disseminate info, distorted). Departmentalization-specialize group of organization based on product, function, clients or location (efficiency vs lack of coordination / cohesion b /groups) Graphic representation of organization's structure. It helps determine span of control and chain of command depicts horizontal and vertical relationships. Mission Statement: what drives the organization's purpose should be written and easily accessible. Helps Determine how employees view their jobs and how they relay that to customer (friendly and fun Vs strict).

CENTRALIZATION SUPPORTS FOCUSED VISION

Vision is a key trait of effective leadership and having a more centralized structure keeps all levels of an organization focused on one vision or purpose. A company president or executive Team can Establish and communicate its vision or strategy to employees and keep all levels moving in the same Direction. This prevents potential inconsistency in vision and helps companies deliver a common Message to customers and communities. Employees have Well-Defined Roles In organizations with strong centralized leadership, employees typically have well-defined job Descriptions and roles. When employees are aware of their duties, as well as the duties and Responsibilities of their co-workers, they are often more likely to be productive and feel more confident in making decisions within their sphere of responsibility. Morale may also improve, as workers may be Less likely to resent each other for either overstepping boundary, on the other end of the spectrum Not working hard enough. When workers have well-defined responsibilities, it can be easier for Management and human resources to determine whether there is a need for creating new roles or hiring more employees. This can help keep costs down by avoiding redundant hires while also making it easier to recruit qualified workers for necessary positions. Who has the decision-making authority in a decentralized organization? Decentralized decision-making is any process where the decision-making authority is distributed Throughout a larger group. It also connotes a higher authority given to lower-level functionaries, executives, and workers. This can be in any organization of any size, from a governmental authority to a corporation. (Robert K. Merton and Alice s. Rossi (1968).

What is the difference between centralized and decentralized authority?

Centralization vs. Decentralization. Organizational structure in business is either centralized or decentralized unlike centralized companies, decentralized companies have less concentrated authority. In a decentralized organization, lower levels in the organizational hierarchy can make decisions.

ORGANIZATIONAL STRUCTURE DEFINITION

Organizational structure is the way responsibility, authority, and lines of communication are arranged. It is also how all processes occur in a company. Additionally, this term is commonly referred to as Organizational culture. The most common organizational structure includes hierarchy with employees Comprising vertical layers of rank where each layer is superior to the layers below and subordinate to the layers above. In addition, most large organizations divide their employees up into subunits called Divisions, departments, segments, business units, (Hyman (1942).

WORK UNITS, OR GROUPS

The objective is to get employees at all levels and across all subunits working towards the goals of the Organization.

ORGANIZATIONAL STRUCTURE MODELS

Models exist on many levels. To simplify the matter, however, they generally fall into two categories: Centralized or decentralized. This main theory is studies across the world.

CENTRALIZATION VS. DECENTRALIZATION

Organizational structure in business is either centralized or decentralized. Thus, centralization and Decentralization are two ends of a spectrum. You can find organizations somewhere along that spectrum. Companies with centralized structure concentrate their authority in upper levels of management. For example, the military has a centralized organization structure. This is because the higher ups order those below them and everybody must follow those orders. Unlike centralized companies, decentralized companies have less concentrated authority. In a Decentralized organization, lower levels in the organizational hierarchy can make decisions. An Example of a decentralized organization is a fast-food franchise chain. Each franchised restaurant in the Chain is responsible for its own operation. Broadly speaking, companies start out as centralized organizations and then progress towards decentralization as they mature. This structure, horizontal when decentralized, places power in the decision maker on the ground floor. Ability of the manager to delegate responsibility. The greater the ability to delegate, the wider the span of organization in general. Amount of interaction and feedback between the workers and the manager. The more feedback and Interaction required, the narrower the span of control. Level of skill and motivation of the workers. The higher the skill level and motivation, the wider the span of control. The final component in building an effective organizational structure is deciding at what level in the organization decisions should be made. Centralization is the degree to which formal authority is concentrated in one area or level of the organization. In a highly centralized structure, top management makes most of the key decisions in the organization, with very little input from lower-level employees. Centralization lets top Managers develop a broad view of operations and exercise tight financial controls. It can also help to reduce costs by eliminating redundancy in the organization. But centralization may also mean that lower-level personnel don't get a chance to develop their decision-making and leadership skills, and that the organization is less able to respond quickly to customer demands. (Merton& Kitt (1950). Decentralization is the process of pushing decision-making authority down the organizational hierarchy, giving lower-level personnel more responsibility and power to make and implement decisions. Benefits Of decentralization can include quicker decision-making, increased levels of innovation and creativity, Greater organizational flexibility, faster development of lower-level managers, and increased levels of job satisfaction and employee commitment. But decentralization can also be risky. If lower-level personnel don't have the necessary skills and training to perform effectively, they may make costly mistakes. Additionally, decentralization may increase the likelihood of inefficient lines of communication, competing objectives, and duplication of effort. (Robert K. Merton and Alice S. Rossi (1968). Several factors must be considered when deciding how much decision-making authority to delegate throughout the organization. These factors include the size of the organization, the speed of change in its environment, managers "willingness to give up authority, employees' willingness to accept more authority, and the organization's geographic dispersion.

Decentralization is usually desirable when the following conditions are met:

- The firm is in a dynamic environment where quick, local decisions must be made, as in many high-tech
- Managers are willing to share power with their subordinates.
- Employees are willing and able to take more responsibility.
- The company is spread out geographically.
- The company is spread out geographically, such as Nordstrom, Caterpillar, or Ford. As organizations grow and change, they continually reevaluate their structure to determine whether It is helping the company to achieve its goals.

Summary Of Learning Outcomes

How can the degree of centralization/decentralization be altered to make an organization more Successful?

In a highly centralized structure, top management makes most of the key decisions in the organization, With very little input from lower-level employees. Centralization lets top managers develop a broad View of operations and exercise tight financial controls.

In a highly decentralized organization, decision-Making authority is pushed down the organizational hierarchy, giving lower-level personnel more Responsibility and power to make and implement decisions. Decentralization can result in faster decision-making and increased innovation and responsiveness to customer preferences. An organizational structure is a system that outlines how certain activities are directed in order to Achieve the goals of an organization. These activities can include rules, roles and responsibilities. The organizational structure also determines how information flows between levels within the Company. Having an organizational structure in place allows companies to remain efficient and focused.

Understanding Organizational Structures

Businesses of all shapes and sizes use organizational structures heavily. They define a specific hierarchy, Within an organization. A successful organizational structure defines each employee's job and how it Fits within the overall system. Put simply, the organizational structure lays out who does what so the Company can meet its objectives. This structuring provides a company with a visual representation of How it is shaped and how it can best move forward in achieving its goals. Organizational structures are Normally illustrated in some sort of chart or diagram like a pyramid, where the most powerful Members of the organization sit at the top, while those with the least amount are at the bottom. Not having a formal structure in place may prove difficult for certain organizations. For instance, Employees may have difficulty knowing to whom they should report. That can lead to uncertainty as to who is responsible for what in the organization. Having a structure in place can help improve efficiency and provide clarity for everyone at every level. That also means each and every department can be more productive, as they are likely to be more focused on energy and time.

CHAPTER 12
RESOLVING TEAM CONFLICT

BUILDING STRONGER TEAMS BY FACING YOUR DIFFERENCES CONFLICT PRETTY MUCH INEVITABLE WHEN YOU WORK WITH OTHERS

People have different viewpoints, and, under the right set of circumstances, those differences escalate to conflict. How you handle that conflict determines whether it works to the Team's advantage or Contributes to its demise. You can choose to ignore it, complain about it, blame someone for it, or try to deal with it through hints and suggestions; or you can be direct, clarity what is going on, and attempt to reach a resolution through common techniques like negotiation or compromise. It's clear that conflict has to be dealt with, but the question is how: it has to be dealt with constructively and with a plan, otherwise it's too easy to get pulled into the argument and create an even larger mess.

Conflict isn't necessarily a bad thing, though, health and constructive conflict is a component of high-Functioning Teams. Conflict arises from differences between people; the same differences that often Make diverse Teams more effective than those made up of people with similar experience. When People with varying viewpoints, experiences, skills, and individuals could achieve. Team members must Be open to these differences and not let them rise into full-blown disputes. Understanding and appreciating the various viewpoints involved in conflict are key factors in its resolution. These are key Skills for all Team members to develop. The important thing is to maintain a healthy balance of Constructive difference of opinion and avoid negative conflict that's destructive and disruptive. Getting to, and maintaining, that balance requires well-developed Team skills, particularly the Ability to resolve conflict when it does happen, and the ability to keep it healthy and avoid conflict in the day-to-day course of Team working. Let's look at conflict resolution first, then at preventing it.

Resolving Conflict

When a Team oversteps the mark of healthy difference of opinion, resolving conflict requires respect and patience. The human experience of conflict involves our emotions, perceptions, and actions; WE EXPERIENCE it on all three levels, and we need to address all three levels to resolve it. We must Replace the negative experiences with positive ones. (Roche W K. Teague P. (2011).

Clarify positions- Whatever the conflict or disagreement, it's important to clarify people's positions. Whether there are obvious factions within the Team who support a particular option, approach or ideas, or each Team member holds their own unique view, each position needs to be clearly identified and articulated by those involved. This step alone can go a long way to resolve the conflict, as it helps the Team see the facts more objectively and with less emotion.

Make sure Good Relationships are a priority

As a manager, your priority in any conflict situation is to take control early and maintain good relationships within your Team. Make sure that everyone understands how conflict could be a mutual problem, and that it's important to resolve it through respectful discussions and negotiation, rather than aggression. Make it clear that it's essential for people to be able to work together happily, effectively and without resentment, so that the Team and organization can function effectively.

Separate People From Problems

At this point, it's important to let Team members know that conflict is rarely one-sided, and that it's Best to resolve it collaboratively, by addressing the problem rather than the personalities involved. The problem is caused by neither person, but they do need to work together to resolve it.

LISTEN FIRST, TALK SECOND

Encourage each Team member to listen to other people's point of view, without defending their own position. Make sure that each person has finished talking before someone else speaks, emphasize that you want to resolve the situation through discussion and negotiation, and ensure that listeners understand the problem fully by asking questions for further clarification. If the conversation becomes heated or your Team members aren't listening to one another, remind them sensitively that it's important to work together and to stay calm. Read our instructions on dealing with difficult people, managing your Emotions at Work, and Dealing with Angry people for more on How to defuse tense situations? (Baba, M L., Glueesing. J. Ratner, H. & Wagner, K. H (2004).

Be sure to focus on work issues and leave personalities out of the discussion. You should also encourage everyone to:

- Listen with empathy, and to see the conflict from each participant's point of view.
- Explain issues clearly and concisely.

- Encourage people to use "I rather that you" statements, so that no one feels attacked.
- Be clear about their feelings.
- Remain flexible and adaptable.

Once you've listened to everyone's needs and concerns, outline the behaviors and actions that you will Or won't tolerate, and gain the opposing parties' agreement to change.

Key Points

Conflict in the workplace can destroy good Teamwork. When you don't manage it effectively, real and legitimate differences between people can quickly get out of control, which can result in an irretrievable breakdown in communication. Use the Interest-Based Relational approach to resolve difficult conflict situations, by being courteous and non-confrontational, focusing on issues rather than individuals, and listening carefully to each person's point of view. You'll find that when people listen and explore the facts, issues and possible solutions carefully, you can resolve conflict effectively. Set up a meeting between the conflicting parties to discuss the issue. Let them know that you are there to work together to find a solution, and that they need to focus on the problem, not the person.

- Ask them to listen carefully to one another's point of view, and to use active listening skills, so that Everyone feels heard.
- Be clear about the facts and then work together to agree on a resolution.
- Get practice by focusing on a relatively mild conflict first, and then try it on a more significant one.

HOW TO MANAGE WHEN VALUES CLASH?

Working Together Despite Different Beliefs

How we behave and how we think, how we solve problems and how we negotiate, how we work and how we play, all of these are influenced by our beliefs and our values. We don't often think hard about the values that matter most to us, but this doesn't mean that they aren't hugely important in our lives. Consider what your most important values are. Honesty, integrity, Fairness, authenticity, and professionalism, for example? Certainly, these are the qualities that we might assume most people would prioritize. But dig a little deeper and you'll likely discover that not everyone shares the same set of values that you do. It might surprise you to learn that the values that matter most to you might barely register with your colleagues. You may even be perplexed by the things that they are passionate about. (Blackburn (2004).

RELIGIOUS OBSERVANCE IN THE WORKPLACE

Treating Faith with Respect

Religious faith is an essential part of many people's lives. It defines their identities and influences the ways in which they live. Sincerely held religious belief can also encourage bonding, mutual understanding, and the development of trust in the workplace, but it can be a flashpoint for conflict, too. For example, otherwise amenable co-workers may respond with hostility if they feel that their faith is not being respected. And people who fail to understand different religions, or the idea of religion in general, may experience unexpected problems and even litigation. This topic lays out the issues around religious observance and helps you to deal with them effectively.

RESOLVING WORKPLACE CONFLICT THROUGH MEDIATION

Managing Disputes Informally

Imagine that you're managing a big project, involving people from a number of different departments. You've made great progress, but tension is mounting between two members of your Team, and what You previously put down to a bit of healthy rivalry, now looks like a full-blown personality clash. At first, you were inclined to leave the situation alone, in the hope that it would run its course naturally. But now your two Team members aren't talking to one another, and you fear that the situation will hinder your project's success if you don't take action. Modern workplaces are complex and comprise people from diverse backgrounds who have different opinions, values and expectations. Add that to the growing need for employees to achieve more with less, and it's not surprising that work-place conflicts sometimes arise. (Tanner F. (2000)

HOW TO MANAGE RIVALRY IN THE WORKPLACE?

Avoiding the Negative Effects of Rivalry

Rivalries can push people to perform at the highest level. They can also encourage them to engage in shocking, and even illegal behavior.

8 WAYS TO STOP SELF-SABOTAGING YOUR SUCCESS

Self-sabotage occurs when your logical, conscious mind (the side of you that says you need to eat Healthily and save money) is at odds with you with your subconscious mind (the side of you stress-eats chocolate and goes on online shopping binges). The latter is your anti-self, that critical inner voice that seems to hold you back and sabotage your efforts. Self-sabotage involves behaviors or thoughts that keep you away from what you desire most in life. It's that internal sentiment gnawing at us, saving "you can't do this." This is really your subconscious trying to protect you, prevent pain and deal with deep-seated fear. But the result of self- sabotage is that we hesitate instead of seizing new challenges. We forget our dreams and goals. In the end, we know we missed out, but we don't understand why. So, what can we do to stop self- limiting behaviors? Here are eight steps you can start taking immediately to stop self-sabotaging your success.

1. UNDERSTAND SELF-SABOTAGE

Many of us are engaged in self-destructive behaviors that have become habits. We allow these Behaviors to continually undermine our success and happiness, but we may not even recognize that we're doing it. Self- sabotage is when we do something that gets in the way of our intent, or of our bigger dreams and goals. We want something, but somehow, we never accomplish it. Why? Because somewhere deep in our subconscious we're fighting against that goal.

Your subconscious probably sees self-sabotage as self-preservation; a way to safeguard and defend yourself, even if it's no longer needed. Some of our self-sabotage is so subtle it's easy to miss. We often fail to recognize how our actions are hurting ourselves. We don't see how our disorganization distracts us, or how we're constantly overthinking all of our decisions, leaving us practically paralyzed with inaction. We don't realize that our reactions to situations end up causing bigger problems in the long run.

2. RECOGNIZE SELF-SABOTAGING HABITS

The first step to breaking the cycle of self- sabotage is becoming aware of these behaviors. Try looking at your behavior as an outsider. What self-destructive habits, patterns and mindsets.

Are you holding you back? Here are few common self-sabotage habits to:

- Procrastination - Instead of tackling an important project in a timely manner, you allow yourself to dawdle to the last minute. It's hard to shine when you don't give yourself time to fix mistakes.

- Negative self-taking/Negative thinking - Your inner dialogue is constantly critical. Are you chastising yourself for past mistakes? Are you constantly criticizing yourself? Be patient

116

with yourself; be kind to yourself. Work to build yourself up.

- Perfectionism - You tell yourself you can't take action until the right time, or believe you need to perfect your skills before you move forward. These are forms of self-sabotage. Perfection is an impossible standard that keeps you from moving forward.

DESTRUCTIVE HABITS HOLDING YOU BACK FROM SUCCESS

Identify Root Causes

Many of us develop unhealthy ways of coping with stress. We repeatedly drop the ball on commitments or fail to take adequate care of ourselves, or we take our relationships for granted. We allow ourselves to react adversely to situations. But sometimes these things are so subtle that we can't see how self-sabotage is at the root of many of our problems. Often, self-destructive habits are rooted in our feelings of inadequacy, even when you're trying to overcompensate by setting high goals for yourself. Some may even use self-sabotage as a twisted form of controlling their own fate. It's better to be at the helm of your failure than having unknown circumstances blindside you. Work on identifying and acknowledging what is causing you to sabotage yourself and then start making changes to stop those behaviors.

Take Time for Self-Reflection

It takes serious self-reflection to understand why you keep shooting yourself in the foot in the First place. Taking the Time to peel back the issues you seem to be inflicting on yourself can lead to a deeper awareness, as well as give you insights into yourself and your underlying Motivations and desires. (Behfar, K., & Thompson L. (2007). The most successful people are those who take the Time to think through their choices, decisions and actions. Successful people learn from what worked or failed to work. They then adjust their course of action by taking a different approach. Only through self-reflection will you gain the necessary insight, perspective and understanding to begin the process of change and transformation.

2 MISTAKES SUCCESSFUL PEOPLE NEVER MAKE TWICE

1. Find Your Inner Positive Voice

Fear is often at the root of what holds us back. We fear that our inner critical voice is right. We start to worry that we don't deserve happiness, aren't tough enough or simply don't have it in us. It's time to put aside those harsh inner voices of "I can't "or "I'm a failure." That negative internal dialogue is a pattern of self-limiting thoughts. Start replacing that critical inner voice with positive, encouraging thoughts. Once you start seeing the areas and ways in which you are limiting yourself, you can start effectively countering that behavior. You can choose to not engage in self-sabotaging behavior. You can start building positive behavior and create an affirmative, confident voice to guide you. (Jehn, KA, & Chatman, J. (2000).

2. Change Your Pattern of Behavior

Changing our negative behaviors is fundamental if we are to stop sabotaging ourselves. In every moment, we're taking action that either moves us toward or away from the person we want to be and the life we want to have. The behaviors you keep permitting yourself to do the ones that are keeping you from what you most desire. Consider how the actions you're taking and the thoughts you're thinking conflict with your happiness and hold you back from your true potential. Then look for ways to replace old patterns with new ones that are more helpful in achieving your goals. At first, we may need to learn to change our behavior by avoiding certain triggers such as negative people or challenging circumstances that cause us to react in Unfavorable ways. If there is a stressful situation that triggers you to react in a negative way, look for ways to bypass or deflect while you learn healthy ways of handling the situation.

FEARS EVERY ENTREPRENEUR MUST OVERCOME

- Make Small, Meaningful Changes

Once you've identified the changes you want to make, pick just one thing that you want to work on. Don't try to make grand, sweeping changes all at once. That's not realistic, and those huge alterations will be hard to maintain and easily given up. Instead, begin by making small, meaningful changes that you'll slowly build to create larger transformations in your life. If you realize you're sabotaging your success by constantly missing deadlines, not following through with leads or simply being disorganized, take a step back and look for one small, meaningful change that you can make to set you on a more successful course. If you're disorganized or constantly getting off track from what you should be doing, take five minutes every morning to tidy your desk and write a to do list. If you're missing deadlines, sit down and come up with a reasonable timeline to get your project done. Then take steps to meet those goals, so you accomplish your objectives and build self-confidence. (Tony Alessandra, Phil Hunsaker (1993).

ACTIONS TO TAKE TO ACHIEVE ANY GOAL

- Set Goals and Make Plans

We often struggle with self-sabotaging behavior when we don't know what to expect. The Unknown can make us feel off-kilter and on unsure footing. Instead of moving forward with confidence, we respond to situations negatively. We allow ourselves to crumble, and then we retreat, feeling incompetent and incapable. The best way to counter this is to lay down solid plans and goals for the future. By having firm, thoughtful plans for each step we take, we will feel more confident about our intentions and what we're doing. You can do this on a daily level, thinking through how you'll respond to situations, people and circumstances. By doing all this, you can take control of your life and banish self-sabotage behavior.

Let me redress to you something regardless procrastination.

Procrastination is about:
- Knowing you should be working on something but putting it off again and again.
- Starting projects, but never quite finishing them.
- Feeling unmotivated or unable to proceed, even when there are lots of exciting opportunities.

CHAPTER 13
ORGANIZATIONAL THEORY

Tell us what is the meaning of Organizational Theory?

O rganizational Theory is the studies organizations to identify the patterns and structures they use to Solve problems, maximize efficiency and productivity, and meet the expectations of stakeholders. What are the key terms of behavior? The key term of behavior is the way a living creature acts. And what is the definition of organizational Behavior?

The definition of organizational Behavior is the studies of the impact individuals, groups, and structures have on human behavior within organizations. It is an interdisciplinary field that includes Sociology, psychology communication, and management. Organizational behavior complements organizational theory, which focuses on organizational and intra- organizational topics, and complements human-resource studies, which is more focused on everyday business practices. Different Types of Organizational Behavior. (Waldo, Dwight (1978). Organizational behavior studies encompass the study of organizations from multiple perspectives, methods, and levels of analysis. "Micro organizational" behavior refers to individual and group dynamics in organizations. "Macro" strategic management and organizational theory studies whole organizations and industries, especially how they adapt, and the strategies, structures, and contingencies that guide them. Some scholars also include the categories of "MESO" scale structures, involving power, culture, and the networks of individuals in organizations, and" field "level analysis, which studies how entire populations of organizations interact. Many factors come into play whenever people interact in organizations. Modern organizational studies attempt to understand and model these factors. Organizational studies seek to control, predict, and explain. Organizational behavior can play a major role in organizational development, enhancing overall organizational performance, as well as also enhancing individual and group performance, satisfaction, and commitment.

Artifacts Values Assumptions

Behavior Model: Diagram of Schein's organizational behavior model, which depicts the three central components of an organization's culture: artifacts (visual symbols such as office dress code), values (company goals and standards) and assumptions (implicit, unacknowledged standards or biases). Topics in Organizational Behavior (Ackerman, M.S. (1996).

Organizational behavior is particularly relevant in the field of management due to the fact that it encompasses many of the issues managers face on a daily basis. Concepts such as leadership, decision making, team building, motivation, and job satisfaction are all facets of organizational behavior and responsibilities of management. Understanding not only how to delegate tasks and organize resources but also how to analyze behavior and motivate productivity is critical for success in management.

Organizational behavior also deals heavily in culture. Company or corporate culture is difficult to define but is extremely relevant to how organizations behave. A wall street stock-trading company, for Example, will have a dramatically different work culture than an academic department at a university.

Understanding and defining these work cultures and the behavioral implications they embed Organizational is also a central topic in organizational behavior.

Organizational Level Theories

Organizational theory draws from various bodies of knowledge and disciplines. Some types of Organizational theories include classical, neoclassical, systems and organizational structure. What are Organizational Theories?

Organizational theory attempts to explain the workings of organizations to produce understanding and appreciation of organizations. These variations on organizational theory draw from multiple perspectives, including modern and postmodern views.

CLASSICAL ORGANIZATIONAL THEORY

The classical perspective of management originated during the Industrial Revolution. It focuses primarily on efficiency and productivity and does not take into account behavioral attributes of employees. Classical organizational theory combines aspects of scientific management, bureaucratic theory and administrative theory. Scientific management involves obtaining optimal equipment and personnel and then carefully scrutinizing each component of the production process, states Stat Pac Inc., an international software development and research company. Bureaucratic theory places importance on establishing a hierarchical structure of power. Administrative theory strives to establish universal management principles relevant to all organizations. (Augier & Teece (2008).

NEOCLASSICAL ORGANIZATIONAL THEORY

Neoclassical organizational theory is a reaction to the authoritarian structure of classical theory. The Neoclassical approach emphasizes the human needs of employees to be happy creativity, individual growth and motivation, which increases productivity and neoclassical approach manipulates the work environment to productivity.

Contingency Theory

Contingency theory accepts that there is no universally ideal leadership style because each organization faces unique circumstances internally and externally. In contingency theory, productivity is a function of a manager's ability to adapt to environmental changes. Managerial authority is especially important for highly volatile industries. This allows managers the freedom to make decisions based on current situations. The contingency theory reveals situations that require more intense focus and takes account of unique circumstances.

Systems Theory

Systems theorists believe all organizational components are interactions other components, according to Stat Pac. Systems theory views organizational dynamic equilibrium, which are continually changing and adapting relationships between organizational components create a complementary theory.

What is Organizational Theory? (Liebowitz (2009).
Organizational Theory (OT) Studies

Everything that is associated with organizations aims to understand organizations and to improve them examines:

- Organizational Design
- Motivation
- Organizational Culture
- Managerial Styles
- Group Behavior
- Leadership
- Communication

Organizational Structure

Why use Organizations?

- Facilitate complex goal accomplishment
- Reduce individual Risk
- Organizational Structure
- Form or Shape of Organization
- Help Coordinate system activity e.g., decision making, communication, etc.
- Organizational Structure is often based on people's implicit theories.
- Structure Organizational Theory
- Organizational Designs
- Factor that impact organizational Designs

Organizational Behavior Movement (Combines classical ORG. Theory with Human Relations Focusing more on structure, less on people). (Botha et al. (2008).

- Organizational behavior seeks to describe, understand, and predict human behavior in the Environment of formal organizations. It recognizes that both the internal, informal Organization (created by human interaction and groups) and the formal organization affect One another, and that management must seek arrangements to maximize the effectiveness of this interaction. Of this interaction.

Organization Theory or Organizational Theory looks at the relationships between organizations and their environment. It also examines the effects of those relationships on how organizations function. It is the study of organizational structures and designs, as well as the behavior of technocrats and managers in organizations. Organization theory also suggests how organizations might be able to cope with rapid change. (Ackoff, R R. L. (1999).

Organizational theories all address several main questions about how a company works?

They assume an organization has structure, goals, and members but focus on the efficiency of the organizations." We can use the theories that match an organization's goals, its personnel, as well as its business environment.

Classical Organization Theory

The classical organization theory emerged at the end of the 19th century. It emerged in the private sector and also in the need for better public administration in the public sector. Both efforts centered on efficiency theories. Efficiency is all about getting the most out of the resources that are available.

WHAT IS ORGANIZATION THEORY?

Everything that is associated with organizations aims to understand organizations and improve them. Organization theory is all about examining organizations and making them better. Classical Theory represents the merger of Administrative Theory. Bureaucratic Theory, and Scientific Management Theory.
Rational System Perspective

The Rational system describes organizations with set goals and formal rules. It concentrates on the Normative structure of organizations. "Normative" means relating to an evaluative standard, i.e., if something is normative, we can evaluate it. Organizational theory is the study of the structures of organizations. Four major theories contribute to this study, classical theory, human relations or neo-classical theory, contingency or decision theory and modern systems theory. Over time, the emphasis in organizational theory has shifted from stiff, hierarchical structures rampant in the industrial age to broader, more flexible structures more prevalent in the technological, modern age.

Contingency/Decision Theory

Followers of contingency theory, also referred to as decision theory, view conflict as manageable. This Theory espouses the principle that organizations act rationally and linearly to adapt to environmental changes. Contingency theory assesses management effectiveness by management's environmental adaptation abilities. In addition, in volatile industries, for example, technology, managers at all levels must have the authority to make decisions in their area, contingent on what is happening. Companies and managers must adjust their managerial styles and techniques based on the conditions occurring around them.

MODERN SYSTEMS THEORY

The foundation of the modern systems theory is the principle that all of an organization's components Interrelate nonlinearly, therefore making a small change in one variable impact many others. A small change can cause a huge impact on another variable or large changes in a variable can cause a nominal impact. Another principle is that organizations operate as open systems in dynamic equilibrium as they constantly adjust and adapt to changes in their environment.

CLASSICAL ORGANIZATION THEORY

There are different theories of organization to predict and explain the process and also behavior patterns in an organizational setting. There are three different types of organizational theory; Classical organization Theory, Neo-classical Organizational Theory, and Modern Organizational Theory. In this composition, we will explore Classical Organizational Theory.

TYPES OF ORGANIZATIONAL THEORY

- Classical Organizational Theory
- Neo-Classical Theory

- Modern Organizational Theory
- System Theory
- Contingency Theory

As the first step towards a systematic study of organizations, the Classical Organizational Theory IS very important. It primarily deals with the anatomy of formal organizations and also views one as a machine and the employees as parts of the machine. Therefore, in order to increase the efficiency of the organization, each employee working in it must become efficient.

6 PILLARS OF CLASSICAL ORGANIZATIONAL THEORY

The main pillars or elements of the Classical Theory are as follows:

1. Division of Labor- In order to obtain a clear specialization in order to improve the Performance of individual workers, the organization must divide work.

2. Departmentalization- The organization must group various activities and jobs into Departments. This allows it to minimize costs and also facilitate administrative control.

3. Coordination- The organization must ensure harmony among diverse functions. This allows it to arrange the group effort in an orderly manner which provides unity of action while pursuing a common purpose.

4. Scalar and Functional processes- A scalar chain is the series of superior-subordinate relationships from the top the bottom in an organization. It facilitates the delegation of Authority or command, communication or feedback, and also remedial action or decision.

5. Structure- Structure is the logical relationship of functions in an organization. Further, these functions are arranged for effective objective accomplishment.

6. Span of Control- This is the number of subordinates that a manager can effectively Supervise. Classical theory has received criticism on several grounds.

Learn more about structure of Organizational here in detail.

Criticism of the Classical Organizational Theory:

- It takes a rigid as well as a static view of organizations.
- Most classical theorists view an organization as a closed system with no interaction with its environment.
- The theory focuses more on the structural and also the technical aspects of organizations.
- It is based on oversimplified and mechanistic assumptions in simple terms, the focus of the Classical Theory is on organization without people.

Therefore, many experts consider it inadequate in dealing with the complexities of an organization's structure and functioning. Also, it offers an incomplete explanation of human behavior in organizations.

1. Division of Labor
2. Departmentalization
3. Coordination
4. Scalar and Functional Processes
5. Structure
6. Span of Control

Why did Classical Theory receive criticism?

The answer is the classical theory views organizations as machines and human beings as parts of the machine. Therefore, classical theorists believed that the efficiency of the organization Improves with the efficiency of human beings. However, this theory takes a rigid and static view of organizations. Also, it focuses more on the structural and technological aspects of an organization with the assumption that it does not interact with its environment. Finally, the theory is based on mechanistic and oversimplified assumptions. These aspects led to the criticism of Classical theory.

What are the different modern organizational design theories?

Modern organizational behavior has become complex. It synthesizes the classical and neo-classical Theories of organization, while incorporating technological development. Modern theories of organization are classified into quantitative theory, system theory and contingency theory.

CHAPTER 14

DIFFERENCE BETWEEN ENTREPRENEURSHIP AND LEADERSHIP EXPLAINED!

Sometimes, an entrepreneur and a Leader, or Say, entrepreneurship and leadership are considered as Synonym, i.e. meaning the same thing. But these two terms have quite different meanings. Entrepreneurship means a set of attributes that an entrepreneur possesses and practices in starting his/ Her enterprises. But leadership is the process of influencing people and providing an environment for Them to achieve the organizational objectives. Thus, leadership is quite different from entrepreneurship. Entrepreneurship can be included in leadership, but not leadership in entrepreneurship.

What is the difference between Entrepreneur & Manager?

Entrepreneurs VS Managers. The main Difference between Entrepreneur and Manager is their Role in The Organization. An entrepreneur is the owner of the company whereas a manager is the employee of the company. Entrepreneurs are risk takers; they take financial risk for their enterprise. By definition the term Entrepreneur is often contrasted with the term "Manager", as they are the key Persons in an enterprise that help in the organization, management, control and administration of the Company. An entrepreneur is a person with an idea, skills, and courage to take any risk to pursue that Idea, to turn it into reality. On the other hand, manager, as the name suggests, is the person who Manages the operations and functions of the organization The key difference between an entrepreneur and manager is their standing in the company. An entrepreneur is visionary that converts an idea into a business. He is the owner of the business, so he Bears all the financial and other risks. A manager, on the other hand, is an employee, he works for a salary.

Traits of a Good Manager

Good Managers are excited about the company where they work and positively communicate to the Employees under them the corporate culture, or reason why the company is unique among others.

Managers can prioritize tasks and lead their department by making tough decisions. But they need to be people oriented as well, not only focused on driving forward the tasks, but listening to employees' concerns and keeping the office on a positive trajectory. Additional character traits which bosses look for in a manager include integrity, honesty and the ability to assume responsibility and hold themselves and others accountable for their actions. (Busenitz & Barney, (1997).

Traits of a Successful Entrepreneur

People become entrepreneurs in part because of their natural ability to look at problems and design solutions. They are highly motivated to bring their ideas to completion and exude a great deal of confidence in their ability. They are not afraid to take risks, financial or otherwise, but also are not fazed by failure when it comes. Challenges that come their way are often seen as a learning experience and perhaps even an opportunity to discover even better solutions. As such, these smart businesspeople are willing to acknowledge when they need more information and are always seeking to learn.

Entrepreneurs are also very passionate about their companies and are willing to work very hard. They Excel at networking with other businesspeople and become skilled at selling their company's products and services. Finally, they must be good managers of money if they are to remain financially successful.

HOW MANAGERS BECOME ENTREPRENEURAL?

Although managers are employees of companies, they can operate in ways that lean toward being entrepreneurial. When managers adapt the traits of entrepreneurs and begin to develop new ideas within the companies where they already work, a concept known as intrapreneurship emerges. It is interesting to compare entrepreneurship and intrapreneurship, as the two are strikingly similar, although they occur within different contexts. In both instances, new products and solutions are Developed, enabling the businesses to grow and expand. However, whereas the entrepreneur takes all the financial risk for such growth, the corporate manager assumes no personal financial risk for his ideas. Entrepreneurs are the starting and ending points of most ideas, whereas managers and employees must communicate their ideas to superiors and then convince senior staff to embrace their ideas and push them forward. Comparison: Entrepreneur refers to a person who creates an enterprise, by taking financial risk in order to get profit. Business startup. And A Manager is an individual who takes the responsibility of controlling the organization. That means ongoing operations. (TC MCDOWELL (2017).

ENTREPRENEUR COMPARISON:

- Primary Achievement
- Motivation
- Approach to task

- Informal Status Owner
- Reward Profit
- Decision Making
- Intuitive Driving Force
- Creativity and Innovation
- Risk Orientation
- Risk Taker

MANAGER

- Power
- Formal
- Employee
- Salary
- Calculative
- Preserving status quo
- Risk Averse

It is important to define the word Entrepreneur one more time. The term "Entrepreneur" is a French origin which means "go between "or "between-takers." An entrepreneur is a person who creates a new enterprise by assembling inputs, land, labor and capital) For production purposes. He assumes all risk and uncertainty, in order to achieve profit and growth of the business venture by identifying new opportunities and combining resources for the purpose of Capitalizing them. He innovates new ideas and business processes. They are classified as innovative entrepreneurs, imitating entrepreneurs, Fabian entrepreneurs, drone entrepreneurs. Further, they can be classified on the basis of business, technology, motivation, area, stages of development, etc.

The Characteristics of a successful entrepreneur are given below:

- Commitment and Conviction
- Capacity to analyze
- Initiative and Independence
- High Personal Efficiency

- High need for achievement

Definition of Manager

By the term "Manager" we mean a person who gets the things done through his subordinates, with the aim of accomplishing business objectives efficiently and effectively. The five primary functions of a manager are planning, organizing, directing and motivating, Coordination and control. The manager is in charge of the particular division, unit or Department of the company. He may directly command workers, or he may direct the supervisors, who will command workers. Therefore, he is the one under whose supervision, his subordinates work and report to him. Managers can be top level managers, middle-level managers, low-level managers. (Drucker, P. F (1985).

The difference between entrepreneur and manager can be drawn clearly on the following grounds:

1. A person who creates an enterprise, by taking a financial risk in order to get profit, is called an entrepreneur. An individual who takes the responsibility of controlling and administering the organization is known as a manager.
2. An entrepreneur focuses on business star up whereas the main focus of a manager is to manage ongoing operations.
3. Achievements work as a motivation for entrepreneurs. On the other hand, the primary Motivation is the power.
4. The manager's approach to the task is formal which is just opposite of an entrepreneur.
5. An entrepreneur is the owner of the enterprise while a manager is just an employee of the company.
6. A manager gets salary as remuneration for the work performed by him. Conversely, Profit is the reward for the entrepreneur.
7. An entrepreneur's decisions are driven by inductive logic, courage, and determination; That is why the decision making is intuitive. On the contrary, the decision making

of a manager is calculative, as they are driven by deductive logic, the collection of Information and advice.

8. The major driving force of an entrepreneur is creativity and innovation. As against this, A manager maintains the existing state of affairs.

9. While an entrepreneur is a risk taker, the manager is risk averse. After reviewing the above points, it is quite clear that entrepreneur and manager are two different people in an organization. So, they cannot be Juxtaposed. While managers are concerned with managing available resources, entrepreneurs focus on spotting and capitalizing opportunities. For an entrepreneur, the main motivation is finding ways to ease the lives of people, to find solutions to problems, to explore what's previously left unexplored.

The Motivation of a Businessman

Most of the people have a misconception that the terms businessman and entrepreneur, carry the same meaning Due to which they use them interchangeably, I won't say that they are wrong, in the long run, an entrepreneur becomes a business, but there is a difference. Even the terms will sound same for a layman, but there is a fine line amidst the two. A businessman walks on the defined path, but an entrepreneur believes in making his own path, which becomes a guideline for another businessman. In this project, we will help you know the difference between businessman and entrepreneur. A person who is engaged in carrying out any activity in the market as for the existing business. When it Comes to originality of ideas, most of the businessmen go for a business which is highly in demand, or Which can make huge profits for them irrespective of uniqueness. A businessman faces tough competition because there are hundreds of rivals already existing in the market undertaking the same business. Although the risk factor is low because he walks on a path that is already tested by the rivals, so the chances of failure are relatively low. The main objective of a businessman of conducting the economic activities is to generate revenue by employing the human, financial and intellectual resources.

By virtue of this, customers are treated as the king of business by the businessman.

Entrepreneur: An entrepreneur is a person who conceives a unique idea or concept to start an Enterprise and brings it into reality. He is the person who bears risks and uncertainties of the business. The venture established by the entrepreneur is known as start up company, which is formed for the very first time regarding the idea, innovation or business process. They are the ones who lead the market always no matter how many competitors will come later, but their position will remain untouched. In economics, the entrepreneur is considered as the most important factor of production, which assembles and mobilizes the other three factors of production, land, labor and capital.

In the long run, these entrepreneurs become a businessman. Entrepreneurs are known for their creative approach. They introduce innovation and coordinate resources. They offer such products and services which bring about a change in the world. A Businessman is a businessman, but an entrepreneur is an entrepreneur, an organizer, a risk taker, a manager at the same time. The former focuses on competition, but the latter gives emphasis on coordination and cooperation of all the resources.

Now let us talk about Businesspeople and entrepreneurs have many similarities. They both provide jobs for the unemployed, give solutions to consumers, and help in developing the economy of a certain nation. However, they are not the same kind of people. A person who is engaged in carrying out any activity, related to commercial and industrial purposes is known as Businessman. A businessman faces tough competition because there are hundreds of rivals already existing in the market undertaking the same business. Although the risk factor is low because he/ she walks on a path that is already tested by the rivals, so the chances of failure are relatively low. An entrepreneur is a person who conceives a unique idea or concept to start an enterprise and brings it into reality. He or she is the person who bears risks and uncertainties of the business. Entrepreneurs are known for their creative approach. They introduce innovative and coordinate the resources. They offer such products and services which bring about a change in the world. Project Management is better when it is visual. Manage all your projects and tasks in one place. Easily collaborate with your Team. I believe Entrepreneurship covers down a lot more meaning than innovation., and innovating something requires typical knowledge and depth about a depth about the subject, shaping in a way so that common people would be helpful or would understand, hence implementing an innovation to a practical Zone and giving this an impact to the society around us is partially called entrepreneurship. It does not necessarily mean what we display in our product has to be innovated rather it has to be new, unique and efficient. There are lot of differences as such There is a broad line between Innovation and entrepreneurship. Innovation is one of the main qualities for entrepreneurship. A person engaged in the same business over the years means that this person has no entrepreneurship qualities. Bringing innovation adds value to his or her business.

CHAPTER 15

LEADERSHIP EXCELLENCE

A leader is far more than a label. Leadership is about taking actions to create sustained, positive Transformations within an organization. Great leaders align their own values and vision with those of Their business and help operationalize them for the future. The most meaningful way to demonstrate these skills is to passionately communicate your shared vision and practice what your company stands for. Leaders also cultivate committed employees who strive to lead as well. It is this approach to leadership that is responsible for The Walt Disney Company legacy known around the world today.

CORE LEADERSHIP THEORIES

Why are some leaders successful, while others fail?

The truth is that there is no "magic combination" of characteristics that makes a leader successful, and Different characteristics matter in different circumstances. This doesn't mean, however, that you can't Learn to be an effective leader. You just need to understand the various approaches to leadership, so that you can use the right approach for your own situation. One way of doing this is to learn about the core leadership theories that provide the backbone of our current understanding of leadership. We explore these in this project. Our Project on Leadership Styles explores common leadership styles that have emerged from these core theories. These include the "Transformational leadership" style, which is often the most effective approach to use in business situations. (American psychology Association (2014) You can also use the Leadership process Model, to understand how your situation affects other factors that are important for effective leadership, and how, in turn these affect your leadership. Power and influence theories of leadership take an entirely different approach, these are based on the Different ways that leaders use power and influence to get things done, and they look at the leadership Styles that emerge as a result. The model suggests that using personal power is the better alternative, and that you should work on building expert power (the power that comes with being a real expert in The job) because this is the most legitimate source of personal power. Another leadership style that uses power and influence is transactional leadership. This approach assumes that people do things for reward and for no other reason. (Drickhamer, D. (2004) Therefore, it focuses on designing tasks and reward structures. While this may not be the most appealing leadership strategy in terms of building relationships and developing a highly motivating work environment, it often works, and leaders in most organizations use it on a daily basis to get things done. Autocratic leaders make decisions without consulting their Teams. This style of leadership is considered Appropriate when decisions need to be made quickly, when there is no need for input, and when Team agreement isn't necessary for a successful outcome. Democratic leaders allow the Team to provide input before making a decision, although the degree of input can vary from leader to leader. This style is important when Team agreement matters, but it can be difficult to manage when there are lots of different perspectives and ideas. Laissez- faire leaders don't interfere; they allow people within the Team to make many of the decisions. This works well when the Team is highly capable, is motivated, and doesn't need close supervision. However, this behavior can arise because the leader is lazy or distracted; and this is where this style of Leadership can fail. Clearly, how leaders behave affects their performance. Researchers have realized, Though, that many of these leadership behaviors are appropriate at different times. The best leaders are those who can use many different behavioral styles and choose the right style for each situation.

Our project "Laissez-Faire" versus Micromanagement looks at how you can find the right balance between autocratic and laissez-faire styles of leadership, while our project on the Blake-Mouton managerial Grid helps you decide how to behave as a leader, depending on your concerns for people and for production. (Kanji, GK (1998).

CONTINGENCY THEORIES, HOW DOES THE SITUATION INFLUENCE GOOD LEADERSHIP?

The realization that there is no one correct type of leader led to theories that the best leadership style depends on the situation. These theories try to predict which style is best in which circumstance. For instance, when you need to make quick decisions, which style is best? When you need the full Support of your Team, is there a more effective way to lead? Should a leader be more people-oriented or task-oriented? These are all questions that contingency leadership theories try to address. Al Dridge, MD & SWAMIDASS, PM (1996). Transformational leaders show integrity, and they know how to develop a robust and Inspiring vision of the future. They motivate people to achieve this vision, they manage its delivery, and they build ever stronger and more successful Teams. However, you'll often need to adapt your style to fit a specific group or situation, and this is why it's useful to gain a thorough understanding of other styles. Our project on Leadership styles takes a deeper look at the different styles that you can use.

Key Points

Over time, several core theories about leadership have emerged. These theories fall into four main categories:

1. Trait Theories

2. Behavioral Theories
3. Contingency Theories
4. Power and Influence Theories

"Transformational leadership," is the most effective style to use in most business situations. However, you can become a more effective leader by learning about these core leadership theories, and understanding the tools and models associated with each core leadership theories, and understanding the tools and models associated with each one. This site teaches you the skills you need for a happy and successful career; and this is just one of many tools and resources that you'll find here at Mind tools.

LEADERSHIP THEORIES

There is a wide and ever-growing variety of theories to explain the concept and practice of leadership. I will provide a brief overview of the more dominant or better-known theories. I hope that others will share their thoughts on whether this list neglects any theories of note. In the future we can discuss some of the emerging leadership theories/ approaches such as adaptive, authentic, and appreciative. It is important to note that this submission attempts to provide an overview of leadership theories versus models. (Adair, J. (1988). I view models as attempts to functionalize the more theoretical aspects of leadership and make them easier to put into play by organizations and consultants. This is, in and of itself, an important activity.

Most theories view leadership as grounded in one or more of the following Three perspectives: leadership as a process or relationship, leadership as a combination of traits or personality characteristics, or leadership as certain behaviors or, as they are more commonly referred to, leadership skills. In virtually all of the more dominant theories there exists the notion that, at least to some degree, leadership is a process that involves influence with a group of people toward the realization of goals. I will say on the front end that, in my opinion, leadership is a dynamic and complex process, and that much of what is written these days tends to oversimplify this process. My goal here is to provide an overview that keeps things simple, without crossing into oversimplification, and for the most part refraining from any critiquing of the various theories. I will leave that to my fellow bloggers for now.

TRAIT THEORY

This theory postulates that people are either born or not born with the qualities that predispose them to success in leadership roles. That is, that certain inherited qualities, such as personality and cognitive ability are what underlie effective leadership. There have been hundreds of studies to determine the most important leadership traits, and while there is always going to be some disagreement, intelligence, sociability, and drive (aka determination) are consistently cited as key qualities.

SKILLS THEORY

This theory states that learned knowledge and acquired skills/abilities are significant factors in the Practice of effective leadership. Skills theory by no means disavows the connection between inherited traits and the capacity to be an effective leader, it simply argues that learned skills, a developed style, and acquired knowledge, are the real keys to leadership performance. It is of course the belief that skills theory is true that warrants all the effort and resources devoted to leadership training and development. (Alimo-Metcalfe, B., Alban-Metcalfe, J. (2005).

SITUATIONAL THEORY

This theory suggests that different situations require different styles of leadership. That is, to be effective in leadership requires the ability to adapt or adjust one's style to the circumstances of the situation. The primary factors that determine how to adapt are an assessment of the competence and commitment of a leader's followers. The assessment of these factors determines if a leader should use a more directive or supportive style.

CONTINGENCY THEORY

This theory states that a leader's effectiveness is contingent on how well the leader's style matches a specific setting or situation. And how, you may ask, is this different from situational theory? In situational the focus is on adapting to the situation, whereas contingency states that effective leadership depends on the degree of fit between leader's qualities and style and that of a specific situation or context.

PATH-GOAL THEORY

This theory is about how leaders motivate followers to accomplish identified objectives. It postulates that effective leaders have the ability to improve the motivation of followers by clarifying the paths and removing obstacles to high performance and desired objectives. The underlying beliefs of path-goal theory (grounded in expectancy theory) are that people will be more focused and motivated if they believe they are capable of high performance, believe their effort will result in desired outcomes, and believe their work is worthwhile.

TRANSFORMATIONAL THEORY

This theory states that leadership is the process by which a person engages with others and is able to create a connection that results in increased motivation and morality in both followers and leaders. It is often likened to the theory of charismatic leadership that espouses that leader with certain qualities, such as confidence, extroversion, and clearly stated values, are best able to motivate followers. The key in transformational leadership is for the leader to be attentive to the needs and motives of followers in an attempt to help them reach their maximum potential. In addition, transformational leadership typically describes how leaders can initiate, develop, and implement important changes in an organization. This theory is often discussed in contrast with transactional leadership. (Bass, B.M. (1985).

TRANSACTIONAL THEORY

This is a theory that focuses on the exchanges that take place between leaders and followers. It is based in the notion that a leader's job is to create structures that make it abundantly clear what is expected of his/her followers and also the consequences 9i.e. rewards and punishments) for meeting or not meeting these expectations. This theory is often likened to the concept and practice of management and continues to be an extremely common component of many leadership models and organizational structures.

SERVANT LEADERSHIP THEORY

This conceptualization of leadership reflects a philosophy that leaders should be servants first. It suggests that leaders must place the needs of followers, customers, and the community ahead of their own interests in order to be effective. The idea of servant leadership has a significant amount of popularity within leadership circles, but it is difficult to describe it as a theory in as much as a set of beliefs and values that leaders are encouraged to embrace.

LET US TALK ABOUT THEORIES OF MOTIVATION AS A LEARNING OBJECTIVES!

After reading this chapter, you should be able to do the following:

1. Understand the role of motivation in determining emploeyee performance.
2. Classify the basic needs of employees.
3. Describe how fairness perceptions are determined and consequences of these perceptions.
4. Understand the importance of rewards and punishments.

5. Apply motivation theories to analyze performance problems.

What inspires employees to provide excellent service, market a company's products effectively, or achieve the goals set for them? Answering this question is of utmost importance if we are to understand and manage the work behavior of our peers, subordinates, and even supervisors.

Put a different way, if someone is not performing well, what could be the reason? Job performance is viewed as a function of three factors and is expressed with the equation below:

- Performance
- Motivation
- Ability
- Environment

Performance is a function of the interaction between an individual's motivation, ability, and Environment. (Bennis W. (1994). Motivation is one of the forces that lead to performance.. Motivation is defined as the desire to achieve a goal or a certain performance level, leading to goal directed behavior. When we refer to someone as being motivated, we mean that the person is trying hard to accomplish a certain task. Motivation is clearly important if someone is to perform well; however, it is not sufficient. Ability or having the skills and knowledge required to perform the job is also important and is sometimes the key determinant of effectiveness. Finally, environmental factors such as having the resources, information, and support one needs to perform well are critical to determine performance. At different times, one of these three factors may be the key to high performance. For example, for an employee sweeping the floor, motivation may be the most important factor that determines performance. In contrast, even the most motivated individual would not be able to successfully design a house without the necessary talent involved in building quality homes. Being motivated is not the same as being a high performer and is not the sole reason why people perform well, but it is nevertheless a key influence over our performance level. So, what motivatespeople?? Why do some employees try to reach their target and pursue excellence while others merely show up at work and count the hours? As with many questions involving human beings, the answer is anything but simple. Instead, there are several theories explaining the concept of motivation. We will discuss motivation theories under two categories: need-based theories and process theories. Secret to customer loyalty is to make a corporate culture of caring a priority. This is reflected in the company's 10 core values and its emphasis on building a Team and a family. (Bryman, A. (1996).

1. What potential organizational changes might result from the acquisition by Amazon?
2. Why do you think Zappos' approach is not utilized more often? in other words, what are the challenges to these techniques?
3. Why do you think Zappos offers a $2,000 incentive to quit?
4. Would you be motivated to work at Zappos? Why or why not?

Theories of Motivation
Learning Objectives

1. Explain how employees are motivated according to Maslow's hierarchy of needs?
2. Explain how the ERG (existence, relatedness, growth) theory addresses the limitations of Maslow's hierarchy?
3. Describe the difference among factors contributing to employee motivation and how these differ from factors contributing to dissatisfaction?
4. Describe need for achievement, power, and affiliation, and identify how these acquired needs affect work behavior?

The earliest studies of motivation involved an examination of individual needs. The seven habits provided are discussed by 7 habits of financially successful people. They want to be financially successful? We will need a lot of drive, knowledge, and dedication to manage our money well enough to develop financial security and independence, but the good news is that it's completely possible. In discussing a good relationship with money. People who are financially successful are actively involved with their money & they understand what their assets are doing. They have budgets, they track spending, they ensure they regularly contribute to investments, and they plan ahead to avoid financial pitfalls. If a financially successful person runs into a roadblock, they work to solve the problem rather than ignoring it or blaming it on something else. This is difficult to do if we have a bad attitude or relationship with finances. We cannot ignore our financial problems and hope they will go away on their own or blame money for problems in other areas of our life. Work to erase our negative or inaccurate money scripts so we too can develop a good relationship with money. Keep a positive attitude and take personal responsibility for our financial situation (even if we have been dealt a tough hand).

7 Habits-financially-successful people. We can develop them for ourselves. 'too many people spend money they haven't earned, to buy things they don't want, to impress people they don't like. Financially successful people don't below their means so that they can invest their money and increase their wealth.

Area of Weakness

Why should our Team determine our weaknesses? Most people answer that the Team needs to correct weaknesses in order to remain competitive and effective. The real reason our Team should determine what our weaknesses are to get them out in the open, with everyone in basic agreement that these are actually weaknesses, so the Team can determine what to do about each one if anything. Why wouldn't our Team want to address and correct each weakness? There are other considerations which must be taken into account. Az a-(4) highly competent, the candidate provides a logical evaluation, with substantial support of 3 strengths of the candidate's leadership practice using a scholarly leadership theory.

The theory behind the book is that each adult individual possesses a certain number of fixed universal personal-character attributes defined by the authors as " Talent themes", Which, together, result in an individual's tendency to develop certain skills more easily and excel in certain fields in a sustainable way while falling or not being able to sustain success or high levels of effectiveness in other fields.

1. Achiever, one with a constant drive for accomplishing tasks.
2. Activator, one who acts to start things in Motion.
3. Adaptability, one who is especially adept at accommodating to changes in direction/plan.
4. Analytical, one who requires data & or proof to make sense of their circumstances.
5. Arranger, one who enjoys orchestrating many tasks and variables to a successful outcome etc.

AZB – Personal Leadership weaknesses. It is hard sometimes when engaging minimally. We can pick 3 weaknesses for example:

1. Conquered the weakness. "Be prepared to share an example of a previous failure or weakness that we have successfully turned into a strength.
2. Be prepared for an interview job questions. Especially tricky ones like this. Thing about our weaknesses ahead of time, but don't rehearse a respond. Our answer might change slightly according to the rest of the conversation with the hiring Manager, and we don't want it to come across as unauthentic or staged.
3. Work-related weaknesses. "Always make sure that they are business appropriate, says someone". Personal weaknesses are okay sometimes, but what these guys are really looking for are our weaknesses in the work-place and how we have overcome them.

AZ-D SMART GOALS-

1. Measurable

When we measure our progress, we stay on track, reach our target dates, and experience the Exhilaration of achievement that spurs us on to continued effort required to reach our goal. To Determine if our goal is measurable, ask questions such as: How much? how many? how will We know when it is an accomplished?

2. Realistic

To be realistic, a goal must represent an objective toward which we are both willing and able to work. A goal can be both high and realistic; we are the only one who can decide just how high our goal should represent substantial progress. A high goal is frequently easier to reach than a low one because a low goal exerts low motivational force. Some of the hardest jobs we ever accomplished actually seem easy simply because they were a labor of, we love. (Avery, G. C. (2005) Criterion score Zero (0)

The company that we work for, needs more attention in order to help it progress. The key to making progress in the work -place or the company and in one's career is to identify and take on developmental assignments. These are roles & activities that provide opportunities to learn new skills, expand our knowledge base, try new behaviors and improve on weaknesses etc.

Azd1- Specific Actions- competent

The candidate provides a logical discussion, with adequate detail, of at least 2 specific actions that will be taken to reach each of the Smart goals discussed in part AZD- Specific Action, the action of a person as a direct form, indeed, a careful reading of the communication and promises to the work-place or to the company. Meet standard take note handout.

A2C- Recommendation for personal Leadership

The factor of effective leadership, as opposed to the authority vested in position or status. The qualities and experience of the individual leader matter etc.

3. Competent

The candidate provides an appropriate recommendation, with adequate support, of 3 theory-based changes to maximize success in managing organizations and leading people in the future, using the same scholarly leadership theory used in part A2a. (Conger, J.A. (1989) Criteria score zero (0)

Theories Of Leadership

Leadership theories distinguish characteristics of particular kinds od Leader. Leadership theories focus on determining specific qualities, such as skills levels, which separate a leader from a follower.

The most common leadership theories include the following trait, contingency, situational, behavioral, transformational, transactional, and participative etc.

CHAPTER 16
LEADERSHIP EXCELLENT &
LEADER BURN OUT

The Key Issues

After spending 19 days in 10 cities with visionary leaders wanting to up their game and achieve more With the organizations they lead. I have heard the issues, they are mostly the same issues challenging Nonprofit leaders and clergy all over the U.S. Here are the top issues these leaders are facing:

- Leader Burn out: Leaders are working too much, giving too much energy and time for too little pay and not about to get everything done.

- Unsatisfactory Board Functioning : Some boards are working out better than others, however, none of the boards are functioning at a level that either the leader or the board members consider optional. (James MacGregor Burns (1978).

- Gaps in Income: There were no organizations with representatives in attendance that were satisfied with their level and consistency of income. Lack of revenue was a challenge that compromised most of the organizations attending. This is also what I have experienced and my 37 years of working with charities.

- Boring, Unproductive Meetings: Every body agreed that meetings were the biggest team killer and that nobody was happy with the process. It is time for a change.

LEADERSHIP EXCELLENCE

Syner Vision Foundation is purposed with providing high quality, relevant content for social Benefit leaders at a cost that's practical. We are introducing a group Mastermind process that's a live and interactive process to work through the major themes and to build support systems for you the non-profit Executive, president, Chairman, or Clergy. We are currently accepting, applications for several groups, which will begin in early September, so it is time to prepare for the experience and start changing the future.

The common factor with successful leader is clarity of vision, ability to articulate that vision, Ability to surround themselves with high performing Teams, and the ability to influence Others to implement the plan to achieve that vision. As the quote Clearly states, it will begin at once, so, what wait?

What's you Get?

Participants in each group will receive the following:

- Personal mentoring by hugh Balou
- A solid work plan with content and templates, we are always connected
- Hugh's intensive leadership material for every facet of development and strategy
- Group synergy for problem solving and collaboration
- Systems and structures for immediate implementation
- Ongoing support both live and virtual.

What's the Fee?

Well, the value is priceless, however there is a monthly fee. Commitment to the journey is important. Transformation is possible first if the leader is open to learning and is committed to transformation. Starting the journey is immediate. Many of the concepts and systems are immediately implementable. However, sustainability is accomplished over time. Only those committed to their own transformation and success are a fit for this program. The content alone is something I change thousands of dollars for. This group masterminds a fraction of those fees and is designed to create immediate results and to build Sustainable transformation over the long-term. Programs are designed to fit the needs of the leader and the organization's budget.

What can I Expect?

First, you will regain your life and your sanity. We will no longer buy into the concept that we must work miracles for little pay and work all the time. Second, you will learn how to influence others to create a "new Architecture of Engagement" so that everyone needs to learn the architecture with more attention to achieve the dream. (McCormack N, Cotter C. Chandos Publishing; (2013)

When talking about Burnout, it is usually defined as a state of physical, emotional and mental exhaustion that results from long -term involvement in work situations that are emotionally demanding. A great deal of research has been devoted to the understanding of factors contributing to burnout has in the cost and the quality of the provided healthcare. Many researchers believe that in difficult and stressful working conditions the work environment should be changed in order to reduce burnout levels successfully, indeed, recent studies have highlighted the role of human resources management in burnout. It has been widely recognized that human resource management policies should be at the core of any sustainable solution that aims to increase health care systems' performance and efficiency.

To conclude, Motivation, leadership, empowerment and confidence are very important factors that should be considered in this direction because they are strongly related with burnout levels.

Leadership Accountability

"There is no such thing as autonomous delegated authority. All delegated authorities are under God's authority. This is why, when scripture addresses those under delegated authority, it also addresses those in delegated authority in the same passage and reminds them of their responsibilities before God." We take this qualification to mean that, just as members are accountable to leaders when it comes to home church ministry, leaders are accountable to the elders or "overseers '(1 Tim. 3; Tit. 1) of the church and to each other. This accountability includes demonstrating to their colleagues that they conduct their ministry in accordance with ministry standards established by the eldership and the servant Team. When Xenos leaders are out of line, members can contact the office to complain to a grievance board, to the relevant sphere leader, or to the elders. They will launch an investigation of leadership errors or misbehavior and give members a full opportunity to be heard.

Leadership Limitations

"The scope of the authority is limited to the area of the authority given to them by God. God does not Require us to obey leaders outside the legitimate sphere of their authority. This is why wives are urged to "be submissive to your own husbands ", not to all men (1 pet. 3 :1; Eph. 5: 22) For the same reason, it is inappropriate for parents to tell their adult children whom they must marry, or for civil authorities to tell their citizens what religious beliefs they must hold, or for church authorities to tell Christians what jobs they may take." (Patient Education and counseling (2010, 78 (2):184-190. (PubMed) (Google scholar).

In connection with point #2, we remember that Xenos has been troubled at times in its past by leaders and members assuming that church leaders have authority in areas where they do not. As a result of Such misunderstanding, members or leaders have at times tended to make leaders into surrogate Parents who regulate areas of life completely unrelated to church ministry. In the Bible, the church is Sometimes called the family of God, but we should remember that the parents are God the father leaders are brothers and sisters like the rest. We notice two exceptions:

1. Paul compares himself to a mother nursing and a father to the Thessalonians according to 1 Thess. 2:7-11. however, the similarity with mothers is the affection they have for their children, and the similarity to fathers was in the way they were "exhorting and encouraging and imploring "the Thessalonians. These actions suggest pleas, not commands.

2. He calls himself the Corinthians' father according to 1 Cor. 4: 15 and implies that this gives him a measure of authority, but this applies only to those who were actually converted through his ministry. (Archives of Hellenic Medicine. (2008).

When talking about Leadership Burnout: Simple way to Reengage the power of mediation. All too often, we as leaders lose our way. Rather than face into what is most important, we allow ourselves to get Pulled into the surrounding chaos or distracted by the "emergency of the day" while the truly How to important matters are left unattended. And, over time, we can begin to feel as though this is simply the way it is, even as we also notice a sense of loss, anger or frustration. We know that we are failing to lead with the kind of excellence that we are innately capable of exhibiting. Missed opportunities, lack of innovation, ethical mistakes, and loss of productivity can be the result. And that isn't even the end of the story. The personal and professional impact of this day-to-day autopilot existence is burnout and disengagement. We begin to feel as though we are simply going through the motions or barely making it through the day. We lose our passion, our joy and our motivation. We miss our lives and when we are not present for the moments of our life, there is no chance that we can lead with the kind of excellence we need today. This is true whether we are talking about leading our own lives, a Team, an organization, a classroom or medical practice. We simply can't afford to have such widespread disaffection. We live in a time when we need to take advantage of every leadership opportunity that comes our way. So, is there a simple way to begin to support leadership development and cultivate the ability to lead with excellence? Happily, there is. (Managing Burnout in the Workplace. Chandos Publishing; (2013pp. 151-192 (Google Scholar). As an example, we know of cases where members have Asked leaders to "hold them accountable "for their spending. Home church leaders agreed and began going over the member's checkbook each month checking whether they were living up to a budget.

Later, when the member came to resent the leader's oversight of this area, they left the church and reported to a cult watch group that Xenos leaders went over their checkbook each month, including assigning them how much to give to the church of course, the member failed to mention that he had requested this assistance, resulting in an embarrassing and misleading picture of Xenos leaders. However, we also believe the incident never should have happened. When the cult watch group later leveled the charge that Xenos leaders oversee budgets including giving commitments, the elders looked into it and found that they were unable to deny the charge, much to our embarrassment. In this case, leaders had allowed themselves to be drawn into inappropriate authority. How to prevent Executive Burnout and Keep your Leader from unraveling? The answer is that it is concerning when an organization's CEO Starts behaving irrationally or erratically, uses questionable judgment and seems to fall apart. Burnout may be the reason. While pressure is a Part of any job, senior-level positions come with high demands and expectations from a number of stakeholders, employees, customers, boards of directors, shareholders. That can affect a leader's confidence, temper and ability to perform effectively. The good news is that a person can recover from burnout, and it can even be prevented.

As a Leader or Manager how to avoid Burnout?

In certain circumstances you should do Self- care a Necessity for care Managers for instance, coordinating care for vulnerable patients is rewarding and meaningful work, but it can also be Incredibly stressful. Increased caseloads, expanding responsibilities, and greater complexity of patient Needs are some of the major stressors affecting care managers, according to a 2016 article in Professional case Management. (J Transcult Nurs. (2005). Excessive and extended stress can lead to Burnout, a state of exhaustion that impacts a person's emotional, mental and physical wellbeing, as Well as their behavior and productivity. A care manager experiencing burnout might feel empty, hopeless, and cynical as if nothing they do is making a difference. That means guarding against burnout is vital, not just for individual case managers but for the health plans that employ them and the patients who increasingly depend on them. In the United States, those patients often face social and Economic disparities and are among an estimated 117 million adults who suffer from one or more Chronic health conditions and 25 percent who suffer from two or more.

HOW CAN CASE MANAGERS BUILD Resiliency?

There are several steps case managers can take to neutralize or prevent burnout, including:

- Identify the Problem, you can't Your feelings, your behaviors, and your physical health and
- Ask yourself whether you may be experiencing any of the symptoms of burnout. Take action. If you think you are suffering from burnout, accept that it won't go away on its own. You need to take intentional steps to address it including slowing down, getting support and re-evaluating priorities. (Human Resources for Health. (2003),
- Practicing work/life balance setting boundaries, protecting your family and personal time, and investing in relationships

that are important to you are all good strategies in avoiding or addressing burnout. If thoughts about work intrude on your personal time, practice mindfulness and other techniques to bring your focus back to the present. Get outdoors, enjoy a good book, enjoy small activities that help you feel refreshed and at peace.

- Take care of your health taking care of physical health is a beneficial means for building resilience to stress. Changing eating habits, exercising, and sleeping are the first and easiest interventions to make effective changes to prevent burnout and build resiliency.

- Get peer support. Peer support groups are a great way to draw strength and inspire resiliency by connecting with others who understand the challenges of being a care manager. Consider creating a peer support group where members can speak honest and confidentially about their struggles, strategies, and victories as a busy case.

Before conclusion, I would like to talk deeply regarding the organizational Leadership. My question is...

What do you think about organizational Leadership?

My answer is the organizational Leadership is a dual focused management approach that works towards what is best for individuals and what is best for a group as a whole simultaneously. It is also an attitude and a work ethic that empowers an individual in any role to lead from the top, middle, or bottom of an organization. While discussing every component of organizational leadership would be well beyond the scope of this document, five key components of organizational leadership are Identified below.

World View

Organizational leadership requires developing an understanding of your own world view as well as the world views of others. World view is a composite image created from the various lenses through which

Individuals view the world. It is not the same as identity, political, or religious viewpoint, but does Include these things. It incorporates everything an individual believes about the world, combining the Tangible and the intangible. An individual's world view is defined by that individual's attitudes, Opinions, beliefs, and the outside forces the individual allows to influence them. World view is the "Operating instructions "for how the individual interfaces with the world. One who does not take into Consideration how individuals' interface with the world is in a much weaker position to lead these individuals. Furthermore, organizational leadership requires an understanding of the composite worldview of the organization, which consists of the many diverse and sometimes conflicting worldviews of the individuals within that organization.

What about Strengths?

Successful leadership requires capitalizing on strengths and managing around weaknesses. Strength can be defined as consistent, near perfect performance in an activity. An individual should perform an activity at around a 95% success rate in order to consider their performance of that activity a strength.

Strength is not necessary the same as ability: an ability is a strength only if you can fathom yourself Doing it repeatedly, happily, and successfully. The building blocks of strengths are:

- Talents, naturally recurring patterns of thought, feeling, or behavior
- Knowledge, facts and lessons learned
- Skills, the steps of an activity.

Developing strength in any activity requires certain natural talents. Although it is occasionally possible to build a strength without acquiring the relevant knowledge or skills, it is never possible to possess a strength without the requisite talent. The key to building a bona fide strength is to identify your dominant talents and then refine them with knowledge and skills. (Canadian Journal of Nursing Leadership. (1999). One need not have strength in every aspect of a role in order to excel in that role. That excellent performers must be well rounded is a pervasive myth. Excellent performers are rarely Well rounded; on the contrary, they are sharp. One will excel only by maximizing one's strengths, never by fixing one's weaknesses. Excellent performers find ways to manage their weaknesses, freeing them to hone their strengths to a sharper point. Excellent performers do not ignore their weaknesses; they work on them just enough so that they do not undermine strengths.

Tell us something about the Ethics?

Organizational leadership requires ethics. Ethics aids leaders in balancing truth and loyalty, individuals and communities, short-term and long-term, and justice vs. mercy. Ethics is not an inoculation or a compromise. It is a process and a lens by which leaders approach a problem situation. Ethics call on us to be impartial yet engaged. Effective leaders utilize ethics to look for the "hidden alternative" in Ethically questionable situations. It is the compass by which leaders navigate not only right vs. wrong, But also, right.

What is the important thing in communication?

In everything you need to communicate. Communication is a key or is a tool for individuals to interface with one another, with groups, and with the rest of the world. It is not a text, email, phone call, or personal visit: these are methods/ mediums of communication. Effective communication requires an Understanding of the VABES 9 Values, Assumptions, Beliefs, Expectations) of those whom with we Communicate. Understanding someone's World view and VABES enables leaders to acknowledge but look past differences, focus on areas of agreement, and to effectively listen for and hear the messages of others. Leaders are able to move beyond communication barriers (appearance, vocabulary, stutter, Lisp, accent, etc.) and focus on the message of the speaker.

The Word of Leadership what is that mean?

It is often the case that people don't want to be leaders for fear of rejection. Leaders are able to rise Above this natural fear and lead by the example of adding value to an organization. Managers and Leaders are not the same. Leaders possess strategic thinking and not only an understanding of the Vision of an organization, but also the ability to effectively carry out and communicate that vision.

Anyone, anywhere, at any level can be a leader. The cornerstones of leadership are:

- Truth Telling
- Promise Keeping
- Fairness
- Respect for the individual

These four cornerstones combined will determine how the individual leader is perceived by others, and in the case of organizational leadership, perception is reality for all effective purposes. A manager may have been delegated responsibility over many individuals, but in failing to exhibit the Cornerstones of leadership or not possessing the requisite strength, ethics, communication, or grasp of world views, that manager is not a leader. In fact, that manager may very well manage a leader who does possess leadership traits. A Simple test of leadership is to" look behind yourself, do you see anyone following you?" If you do not, you are not a leader! (International Journal of Nursing studies. (2012).

Leaders may employ various methods of leadership. Some of the more important methods are:

- Model the way (set the example)
- Share your vision (enlist others)
- Challenge the process (look for ways to grow)

- Enable others to act (empowerment)
- Set goals/build trust (direction)
- Encourage the heart (positive reinforcement)

Successful organizational leadership includes:

- Working to understand the worldviews of others
- Recognizing and develop your own strengths
- Looking for the "hidden alternative"
- Focus on the message, not the messenger (Journal of Applied Psychology. (1999).
- Appealing the appropriate theories and methods of leadership to a given situation.

To conclude this chapter 16 on Leadership Excellent Leaders and Leadership Teams:

You want to be:

- More effective
- More Relevant
- More Differentiated, and
- Have greater influence to drive results.

In this case find that you are often too committed to the past or too consumed by the Present to plan or implement the changes you know are needed. And, at the same time, realize that in addition to business strategy, you must also develop What you desire in terms of organizational culture, diversity, sustainability, and innovation to inspire greater commitment and loyalty over the long-term? Regarding Leadership excellent you are not alone; you need a new process and a fresh plan and we can help. (Human Resources for Health. (2006). Our Leadership Excellent fast start program is designed to position you and your Team, to take on and succeed in some of the most significant work- place challenges and market-place opportunities facing us today. Our program can also be designed to effectively engage and align you and your HR, marketing, sales, and business development Teams so that you can immediately begin to stand out more throughout the work-place, marketplace, and recruiting space. As leaders, sometimes we just need to regroup and refocus with a fresh perspective and proven approach from someone who has been in our shoes. Our Leadership Excellent growth and Excellent fast start program is designed as a stand-alone half or full-day workshop or modules. Either approach can be customized to supplement your related strategic planning efforts. (Petridou E. Thessaloniki: Zygos; (1998).

Avoiding Leadership Burnout, it is my opinion that we are living through what is probably the toughest era ever to be an educator in The United States, Whether as a class-room teacher or a building administrator. In my travels around the country as an education consultant (who led secondary schools for years), Teachers and school Leaders often engage me in intense discussions about the topic of avoiding burnout. This isn't surprising Considering what educators are now being asked to do. In terms of lifting school achievement, educators are expected to work miracles daily. Whatever the hand that's dealt to the educators of a given school, they are expected to produce, and quickly.

REFERENCES

Tony Alessandra. Phil Hunsaker (19993)

Hogg, Michael A; Terry, Deborah l. (2000-01-01).

Moscovisi, Serge (1980).

Alport, G W. (1961). Pattern and growth in personality, New York: Holt, Rinehart 7 Winston

Baker, S. (1996). "Placing Values Research in a Theoretical Context ", in Elfring, T., Siggard Jensen, H.

Money, A., (Eds.), Theory Building in the Business Sciences, Copenhagen: Handelshoyskolens Forlag.

Beck, D. E. and Cowan, C.C. (1996). Spiral Dynamics: Mastering Values, Leadership, and change;

Exploring the New Science of Meme tics, Cambridge: Blackwell.

Dade, P. (2008). Managing Talented people- Managing Resource: Managing a process of Resourcefulness?

http://www.cultdyn,couk/ART067736u/Managing%20Talented%20people.pdf

Finkelstein, S. and Hambrick, D. (1996). Strategic Leadership: Top Executives and Their Effects on Organizations, St. Paul Minn.: West publishing Company.

Alban-Metcalfe, R.J., & Alimo-Metcalfe, B. (2000). The transformational leadership questionnaire: A Convergent and discriminant validation study. Leadership & Organization Development Journal, 21(6), 280-296.

Einstein, W.O., & LeMere-Labonte, J. (1989). Performance appraisal: dilemma or desire? Sam Advanced Management Journal, 54 (2): 26-30.

Monga, M. l. (1983). Management of performance Appraisal. Bombay: Himalaya Publishing House.

Cooper, R., and R.S. Kaplan. (1991). Profit priorities from activity-based costing. Harvard Business Review 69:130-135

Forrester, J.W. (1961). Industrial Dynamics. Cambridge, Mass.: The MIT Press.

Lawler, E.E. (971). Pay and organizational Effectiveness: A psychological View, New York: McGraw-Hill.

Abowd, J. (1990) Does performance-based management compensation affect corporate performance?

Industrial and Labor Relations Review 43(3): 52-73.

Adams, J. (1965). Inequity in social exchange. Pp. 272-283 in L. Berkowitz, ed., Advances in Experimental social psychology. New York: Academic Press. American Compensation Association (1987). Report on the (1987). Survey of salary Management Practices. Scottsdale, Ariz, American compensation Association.

Effect of Leadership Behavior on commitments

The hypothesis in this study was built "there between leadership behaviors influences on employee Performance. Based on a hypothetical test, leadership behaviors significantly influence on

Commitment with coefficient 0703, p value 0.000 is smaller than 0.05. These results support the theoryof Ying and Zaman (2008). Which states that leadership behaviors affect the commitment.

Allert, J. & Chatterjee, S. (1997). Corporate communication and Trust in Leadership. Corporate Communication, an International Journal, 1: 14-22.

Appelbaum, C. & Hebert, D. and Leroux, L. (1999). Empowerment: power, culture and leadership, a Strategy or fad for the millennium? Journal of Work-place Learning.

Adair, J. (1988). Effective leadership. London. Pan Books.

Bass, B.M. (1985). Leadership and performance beyond expectations. New-York: Free press.

Bryman, A. (1996). Leadership in organizations. In Clegg S. R., Hardy, C. and Nord, W.R. (Eds).

Handbook of Organization studies, pp. 276-292. London: Sage.

Aral, S.& Van Alstyne.M. (2011). The Diversity-bandwidth trade-off. American journal of sociology, 117 (1), 90-171.

Burt, R.S. (2012). Network-related personality and the agency question: Multirole evidence from a Virtual world. American journal of sociology. 118 (3), 543-591.

Awa WL, PLAUmann M. Walter U. Burnout preventions. A review of intervention program. Patient Education and counseling. (2010). 78(20184-190. (PubMed) (Google scholar).

McConmak N. Center c. Chando's publishing; (2013). Managing Burnout in the Work-place (Google scholar).

BIOLOGY

I am an ordained pastor since 1984 by the Mission of Lord Mountain in Port-Au-Prince-Haiti. And have Been Licensed by the State of Haiti and by the Justice palace of Port-Au-Prince. I am a founder Of the First Baptist church of Miragoane, Haiti years of 1978-1984. And I have been certified by the red cross in Port-Au-Prince. And also, I have been ordained and licensed by the Florida Baptist Convention as a pastor. And I am a founder of the Bethany Baptist church in Orlando, Florida and Recently 1 founded a Mission which is HEADQUARTERS OF MISSION "HOPE GLOBAL VISION" Which is having now HOPE GLOBAL VISION UNIVERSITY LLC INCORPORATED In Orlando, Florida. After many reflections I found that it is very Helpful to help people all over the world by Instructing them spiritually and intellectually. Different ages Specially the young people, and teenage etc. I am also a founder of United of Evangelical Leaders of Central Florida in other words Association of pastors.

Teaching Experiences:
Post Secondary:

Teaching languages

1978-198 Port-Au-Prince- Haiti.

Jonas Augustin College

1979-1980- Dean

Martin Luther king College

1983-1985-Professor

Saint-yves College

1978-1980- Professor

Louis-Mercier College

1983-1985----------------

Brother Pierre-Louis College

1978-1985--------------------

Heart of Jesus College

1978-1982----------------------

Amedee Brun College

1977-1981-----------------------

Oswald Durand College

1978-1982-------------------------

Brother Raymond Saintil College 1976-1985 as a founder. Haitian American Institute- P-AU-P- Haiti. English Review by the department of Education. Graduated from Gerard Armand Joseph College of Commerce- in accounting year of graduation 1982.-P-Au-P- Haiti. CITIZENSHIP Bible COLLEGE, Port-Au-Prince, Haiti, Bachelor Degree 1977- 1980.1976- Attending linguistic school of LOPE DE VEGA, Bois-Verna- P-AU-P- Haiti. Law school: American Heritage University -school of Law, U.S.A. California- J.D. Candidate. Keiser University- Orlando, Florida – Associate of paralegal U.S.A. year of graduation – 2006- legal Studies. Barry University- Orlando, Florida- Bachelor of Liberal studies or legal studies – U.S.A. 2009. New Orleans Baptist Theological Seminary- NEW- ORLEANS, LA. – M.DIV. 1992. Nova Southeastern University- Orlando, Florida- U.S.A. 2010-M.B.A..Everglades University- Maitland- Florida- MASTER OF BUSINESS ADMINISTRATION OR GENERAL Business-2015-2017.NOTARY PUBLIC U.S.A. CHAPLAIN NATIONAL & INTERNATIONAL North Central University, U.S.A. Doctor of philosophy In Business Administration or PHD.B.A.

www.ingramcontent.com/pod-product-compliance
Lightning Source LLC
Chambersburg PA
CBHW051311120626
46547CB00015B/2182